THE MESSENGER

green
press
INITIATIVE

THE MESSENGER

Awakening to the Presence of the Other Side

❧

EDWARD TABBITAS

Lantern Books • New York
A Division of Booklight Inc.

2006
Lantern Books
One Union Square West, Suite 201
New York, NY 10003

Copyright Edward Tabbitas 2006

Library of Congress Cataloging-in-Publication Data

Tabbitas, Edward, 1947–
The messenger : messages from the spirit world / Edward Tabbitas.
p. cm.
ISBN 1-59056-100-7 (alk. paper)
1. Spiritualism. 2. Tabbitas, Edward, 1947–3. Mediums—Biography. I. Title.
BF1261.2.T33 2006
133.9'1—dc22
2006009747

I dedicate this book to the Creator God for enhancing my courage to move beyond my fears into the world of spiritual communication.

To Santino Badalamenti

TABLE OF CONTENTS

༄

Do not stand by my grave and weep.
I am not there, I do not sleep.
I am the thousand winds that blow.
I am the diamond glint in the snow.
I am the sunlight in ripened grain.
I am the gentle autumn rain.
When you awake in the morning hush,
I am the swift uplifting rush
Of the quiet birds in circle flight.
I am the soft starshine at night.
Do not stand by my grave and cry.
I am not there. I did not die.

—Author Unknown

And when he shall die
Take him and cut him out in little stars
And he will make the face of heav'n so fine
That all the world will be in love with night
And pay no worship to the garish sun.

—William Shakespeare, *Romeo and Juliet*

ACKNOWLEDGMENTS

I am deeply grateful to my wife, Prudence, and my children, Philip, Jennifer, Anthony, Debra, and Michelle, for their unconditional love and encouragement, and also my grandsons, Anthony Benjamin and Philip Nunzio, for their unconditional love.

My special gratitude with love to my parents and all the loved ones who have passed over and allowed me to communicate with them.

Next, I would like to thank all my family and friends for their encouragement. I am grateful to Terry Murphy for her trusting friendship, patience, understanding, and unconditional inspiration.

From my heart I am indebted to my guides.

Also my thanks to Joan Taccetta and Nina Badalamenti and Gloria Ditillo.

Finally, I would like to thank Gene Gollogly and Martin Rowe. I am very grateful to them for their encouragement and helping me bring this book to full fruition.

PREFACE
by Peter Valentyne

H wise person once said, "When the student is ready, the master will appear." When I first read those words, they felt like a promise that help would come to those who persevered, those who had enough faith to not fold their hand before the game of life could be played for all it is worth. Halfway through my life, I am still determined not to fold.

One evening in early 1999, I found myself at a fund-raiser in which the guest speaker was a man who specialized in "lifting the veil" and conversing with the dead. I finagled one of my friends— an unabashed skeptic—to join me, figuring the evening was sure to be good for a few laughs at least. We both prided ourselves on our good sense and sat waiting for the show to begin, like two mathematicians at a peep show. Although I was primed for a night of cosmic titillation, another side of me secretly longed to be moved by miracles. I began entertaining the notion that the man who was to be the main attraction of the evening would be full of panache, possibly decked out in an exotic turban and a cape full of stars, while my poker-faced accomplice was already thinking up ways to throw the poor guy off his game. We weren't really as antagonistic as all that, just bored and determined to exhibit a "we dare you to impress us" stance. Nevertheless, I could not stop thinking about a loved one I had lost along the way, nor could I ignore the strange appeal that the evening offered.

When the show finally got started and the speaker was introduced, a somewhat slight, rather ordinary-looking man walked out onto the stage. He proceeded to change our lives one by one. To nearly everyone he addressed, he seemed to offer disquieting, if not pertinent, information. Some of the audience members, he noted, were surrounded by loved ones who had crossed over. Some were given messages both public and personal, while others were made aware of psychic problem areas in their bodies. I sat there contemplating what kind of creature this was . . . and what such a burden of knowledge as his might imply. Instead of my usual inner voice saying, "God, I hope he doesn't pick me," I was surprised to find myself silently pleading that he would turn his attention my way. Time and again I watched as he dipped into the fourth dimension with only a subtle movement of his fingers to beckon invisibles to step forward and testify. I was struck by his lack of affectation, glitz, ego or pretense, even while he reminded me of a circus ringmaster or lion tamer, encouraging the ghosts to step up to their marks. Some people laughed nervously when he addressed them, some broke down in tears after measuring the implications of his messages. And then he picked me, and the world went cockeyed.

"Come on down to the stage," he said. I had to obey. I couldn't remember ever being chosen for anything as, without the slightest bit of focus, I made my way from my seat to the stage, stepping on several pairs of feet in the process.

"I want you to think of a color," he instructed. "Think of the color blue."

My world went blue.

"You don't have to feel nervous," he said.

"Yes, I do," I said with a laugh.

At one point he touched my hand, and I was immediately aware that I was a liquid reservoir merely in the guise of a human being. I tried to describe this sensation as best I could to him and the audience.

He asked for a towel to dry the residual wetness from his hands. Everyone laughed.

"I sense some blockage in the throat chakra," he observed.

I wasn't sure what that meant, but it didn't sound good. Still, I was grateful that someone was taking my psychic health seriously. I began praying he would rise up and heal me on the spot.

He went on to explain that the throat chakra is a center for self-expression and communication, and when there is a wounding or suppression in this area the entire body can be thrown off balance. All of this rang alarmingly true, because I had chosen to become a writer in the hope that it would compensate for a fearful reluctance to express myself socially.

That evening was to be the first of many sessions spent in consultation with Ed Tabbitas. He invited me to remain a client even as an irrepressible friendship grew between us. I still marvel that my longing for a master had manifested. Yet, even so, my healer-as-magician expectations were challenged session after session. Ironically, what I would come to realize under his tutelage was that Ed would not be healing me per se, but giving me the tools with which I could heal myself.

INTRODUCTION

"*I* need to ask you something," my mother said to me a few months before she died. "But I don't want you to become upset."

"What do you want to ask me, Mom?" I replied.

"Tell me how to die," she said. "I've never done this before."

Stunned, I could feel a shocked expression come over my face.

"Tell me how to die," she repeated.

At first I didn't know how to answer.

"How am I supposed to know?" I demanded. "I've never died before, either."

"Oh, yes you have," she assured me. "In many past lifetimes."

After hearing those words, I felt comfortable sharing with her the reality that I had known since childhood, a reality filled with spirits of those who have died and who often visit me. For many years I had kept these experiences to myself, out of fear or confusion, or both. But now, with an open invitation to discuss life after death with my mother as she struggled with her second bout of cancer, I felt strangely calm about expressing my view.

I told Mom that when it was her time to leave she should simply walk toward the light and keep on walking. I said that there would be others on the other side to greet her and that she would recognize each person who came to help her. I assured her that she would recognize her "helpers" by the essence they radiated, which was pure love. We discussed the possibility that she would hear the harps of the angels guiding each step she took into the doorway of the light that opens to the heavenly realm. This light, I said, was emitted from the souls who have passed over before, a kind of shower of love.

I explained to my mother that while she was on her journey she would feel the presence of those she left behind, but should not allow our love to hold her earthbound. I assured her that she would let us know when her transition was complete.

From that day, as time passed, our conversations became centered on spiritual issues. Everything that I believed and had witnessed all of my life, my mother was now confirming. Her experiences as she neared death gave me answers to the great mystery of life and death. At times my mind could not believe what my ears were hearing. If there had been no pain involved in her struggle with cancer, I would have been even more grateful for my mother's wisdom. It was only later that I realized that my mother had become my greatest teacher.

Death, for most of us, is perceived as our last and final voyage because we believe that we have never died before. Few of us remember our past lifetimes. Yet each of us has taken part in this special ritual many times before.

From the moment we are born until the age of three we have memories of an angelic realm. It is our connection to the angelic realm that prompts us as young children to laugh and have conversations with people who aren't there. Children sometimes claim they have spoken to a grandparent who passed over, one they may have never met on earth.

Beginning around age three, we replace the light of love from the angelic realm with the artificial light of earth. We forget what we learned in the angelic realm and begin to distrust our neighbors and people of different colors. We imagine them as threats to our lives and take on many fears. Greatest is our fear of dying. Because this is so, it is important for each of us to look at other people for their angelic light. Then we will learn to understand that another person's needs may simply be a manifestation of his fears.

As we move on in this life, on this wonderful earth we all share, we must always try to keep in mind that what we do today may come back to us tomorrow. Usually, we come to realize in our final days that we have to make peace, not only with ourselves, but with our loved ones. We believe that God is going to judge our sins. Many of us do not understand that we are given free will by God, which means that we are also given the burden of judging ourselves. Who better than you to judge the things you may have done wrong? If someone else were to judge us, in time the details

of our transgressions would be forgotten. But if you and I examine ourselves, the personal nature of our judgment can last a lifetime. And at the close of your life, you, like all of us, are apt to
recall all the things you have done wrong, as well as the wonderful things you did for others.

In addition to recalling the actions of this life, there are those
of us who can remember fragments or large portions of other exis-
tences, other lifetimes.

Sometimes we ask Creator God for things that cannot be, or
should not be, and, of course, we are not given them. Many of us
have asked to have the life of our loved ones extended. But it was
the choice of that loved one prior to his birth to leave on that air-
plane on that day. Many times we blame God for taking a loved
one, but do we ever take the time to thank God for bringing that
loved one into our lives?

When we say our prayers, each prayer is heard individually, iden-
tified and answered. Often, the answer does not come at the moment
we would like, or with the result we hoped for, but most certainly
when we need a prayer answered, it will be. If the answer does not
seem satisfactory, you must examine it from the standpoint that God
has provided you with a solution in keeping with your destiny.

In their foreword to Elisabeth Kübler-Ross's book *Death: The
Final Stage of Growth,* Joseph and Laurie Braga wrote:

> All that you are and all that you've done and been is cul-
> minated in your death. When you're dying, if you're fortu-
> nate to have some prior warning (other than that we all
> have all the time if we come to terms with our finiteness),
> you get your final chance to grow, to become more truly
> who you really are, to become more fully human. But you
> don't need to, nor should you, wait until death is at your
> doorstep before you start to really live. If you can become
> to see death as an invisible, but friendly, companion on
> your life's journey—gently reminding you not to wait till
> tomorrow to do what you mean to do—then you can learn
> to live your life rather than simply passing through it.[1]

This is the reason for this book, to show you, through my experience as a "sensitive" and as a spiritual counselor, how to die with purpose, with a sense of accomplishment, and with a strong desire to go forward further than you have been. First, you must come to understand that life is preparation for death. Death is not the end, ever. But because we have never died before in the body we now occupy, we are uncertain, fearful, often depressed and unconvinced that we have a future, that our spirits have a home in a generous domain beyond the scope of our vision.

As a spiritual counselor, I have explained death as I understand it to hundreds of people who have lost a loved one, and every experience has convinced me that we must never fear death nor think of it as an ending. Rather, it is the departure point for the next stage of human growth. In this book, I hope to show how many people have come to embrace this belief through receiving messages from departed loved ones.

As you will discover, I came to spiritual counseling after many experiences with the dead and dying. In retrospect, those happenings were like a trial period in my life, a training for an apprenticeship in the mystery of life and death. Not until I had spent many years as a husband, father, and business owner in the Brooklyn neighborhood in which I was born and raised did I begin to use my abilities to help others. Apart from the floral wedding arrangements and other happenings that come through our flower shop every day, I perform counseling as an ordained interfaith minister and work with students who are developing their own psychic gifts. The purpose of this book is to share my experiences as a clairvoyant, as they developed in my childhood and shaped the person I am today, in the hope that I may shed some light on the nature of this and other psychic gifts. In Part Two, I share the experiences of friends, family, and clients in remarkable stories of hope, courage, and faith. They are stories of those facing death, those learning to say goodbye, and those discovering—without a doubt—that their departed loved ones live on.

1. Elisabeth Kübler-Ross, *Death: The Final Stage of Growth* (Englewood Cliffs, NJ: Prentice Hall, 1975).

PART ONE

Visions and Voices

1. GREAT-GRANDMA LILY

*O*n January 17, 1947, I entered the earth plane. My new family would be my mother, Mary, my father, Philip, and a four-year-old brother, Anthony. Four years later, my sister Connie was born. Next came my sister Carol. We were raised in an apartment in Brooklyn in a predominantly Italian Catholic neighborhood. We were close-knit, spending a lot of time with my mother's parents, who lived near our home in a three-story building. The first level of the building was my grandparents' furniture store. On the second floor resided my great-grandmother, and on the third was my grandparents' apartment.

Great-grandma Lily, who was born in Italy, was a very soft lady with snowy white hair and twinkling blue eyes. I remember the day she passed away. My mother broke into tears when her brother, John, came with the news that Great-grandma Lily was dead. That was the first time I heard the word "death." I was eight years old at the time, and I remember hearing the word "died" without understanding, and I became frightened. I had never seen my mother cry, and her weeping only heightened my fear of the unknown.

Since we children were told that Great-grandma Lily had gone to heaven and would not return, we learned that death meant you just disappeared and were forgotten.

One Sunday, several years after Great-grandma Lily died, our family visited my grandparents. I was sent by Grandma Conchetta to get milk for the coffee always served after dinner. I did not hesitate for a moment, since I was always happy to go into Grecco's Bakery, especially if the baker's daughter, Rosie, was there.

When her parents were absent, Rosie always gave me two cookies—one to eat immediately, and one to go on. On good days,

Rosie gave me rainbow cookies. The wonderful, sweet smells from the fresh breads, cookies and cakes were always tantalizing.

Rosie and her mother were the only people in our neighborhood who still called me by my real name, Nunzio. I didn't mind them using my legal name, but I refused to answer to anybody else who addressed me that way. No one else called me Nunzio. By the first grade, I had decided I would be called Ed.

I was happy to see Rosie behind the counter and asked her for a quart of milk. Along with the milk she handed me two rainbow cookies.

Pleased by Rosie's gift of two cookies and her parting warning, "And Nunnie, don't put the other one in your pocket, it will get squashed," I ran home and headed up the stairs. A quarter of the way up I saw Great-grandma Lily standing on the first floor landing.

As she stood there smiling, hands folded in front of her, my first thought was to go over and kiss her. Then I remembered to be afraid. My parents had told me that she had gone to heaven. I stood frozen on the stairs just staring up at her smiling face. As always, she wore a flowered, one-piece dress. Her white hair, like a snowy cap, was drawn back in a bun behind her neck.

Cautiously, I crept up the stairs, pressing my back against the railing. When I reached the first floor landing, Great-grandma Lily was still smiling as I slipped past her. When I had covered half the distance up, I bolted and raced to the top floor. By the time I clattered to my grandparents' door, I had caused such a commotion that my grandfather rushed into the hallway and started yelling at me. I don't think he paid any attention to my question, "If Great-grandma's in heaven, why is she on the landing downstairs?"

Ignored by my family, I was easily distracted from my fright by the sweets on the table.

Little did I know that I would see Great-grandma Lily on the stairway many times in the years to come.

I remembered her custom of stepping out into the hallway to greet all incoming friends and family. But her habit took on a new meaning after her death. To me, when she appeared, it was a warning that somebody in the family would soon die.

Within a week of seeing Great-grandma standing on the landing for the first time, my father died.

2. THE WISH

As a child I had a speech impediment, which most people call a lisp. My father often teased me about it. He thought that by teasing me I would realize what I was doing and correct what he considered "a lazy way of speaking."

The last time my father teased me was June 11, 1960. I was thirteen and it was Saturday evening. I felt his treatment was so unjust that I ran to my bedroom and wished him dead. I prayed that I would not have to endure his cruelty ever again.

I thought my prayer was answered, because there was no teasing from my father for the next four days. I had forgotten about wishing for his death, until the morning of June 16. My mother was in the kitchen preparing our lunch. I could hear my father calling us for school, since it was eight o'clock. Like most children, we dreaded getting out of bed on school days. He called our names again from the living room. On his second call, I was out of bed. I heard my mother walk into the living room from the kitchen, calling out my father's name with a sudden fear in her voice.

My brother Anthony and I ran into the living room and saw our father slumped over the couch. My mother instructed Anthony to lift and carry him to the window for some air. He rested my father's limp body on a recliner in the dining room near a window. My father called out, "Mary . . ." and gasped a final breath.

My mother was frantic. Anthony told me to go downstairs to the butcher and call for an ambulance. We had no telephone.

Two policeman arrived before the ambulance came. They were very kind to us, and asked me to call the rest of the family to the house to be with my mother. Forty-five minutes later the ambulance finally arrived and the paramedics pronounced my father dead of a massive heart attack.

The paramedics covered my father's body with a sheet. I went into my bedroom and told myself, "If I go back to sleep, I will wake up and find out this is only a dream."

As I lay on my bed, I remembered how I'd wished for my father's death. But at that terrible moment I realized I did not want my father to die; in fact, I didn't even know what death really meant. I would learn all about it within the next five days.

My mother insisted on being present as the funeral director took my father's body away. I did not understand where they were taking him. Peering out my bedroom window I saw two men carrying a long, black bag and watched my mother crying uncontrollably.

The limousine arrived on schedule that evening. My immediate family stepped into the elongated car, which came to a halt after just a few blocks in front of the Aievoli Funeral Home.

We were helped out of the limousine by the same two men who had carried my father from the house. As we climbed the stairway to the funeral home, two large glass doors were held open for us and my mother started to cry again. In the hallway was a black velvet board that stated my father's name, the date, the name of our church, and the place of his burial, Pinelawn National Cemetery, Chapel A. A second set of doors opened for us as if we were going to make a grand entrance. I still did not understand what was happening. Was my father playing a joke?

The doors opened into the largest room I've ever seen, lined with rows and rows of chairs. The walls were blanketed by large floral arrangements.

My mother let out the most piercing cry I had ever heard. As the men who walked ahead of us stepped aside, I finally saw the reason for my mother's scream: it was my father, laid out stiffly in his coffin. Then, whimpering, my mother leaned over and kissed him.

To me, my father, lying in what I believed was a large jewelry box, looked like a young boy at rest, not a man of forty.

My father had blue-black hair. Would I ever see his large charcoal eyes again? Even though my dad was only four feet, eleven inches tall, he was a giant.

Now, death was starting to have meaning for me.

Father was dressed in a black suit with a white shirt and a tie, and he held rosary beads in his clasped hands. The cross attached to the rosary was standing straight up, between his index and middle fingers. His hands rested on a small black Bible. On the right of the casket, placed by his feet, was a floral arrangement shaped like a heart of roses with a banner on which gold script spelled out, "Our Beloved Daddy."

The lid of the casket was cream-colored velvet, and attached to it was a large rosary, composed of the tiniest red roses, fifty-three in all. I knew the number because I counted them. Across the rosary was another ribbon which read, "Our Beloved Daddy."

In the corner, on the left side of the casket just above my father's head, was an American flag folded in the shape of a triangle. By the head of the casket stood an enormous heart of roses, with the script, "My Beloved Husband."

It seemed I stood at the casket for the longest time, yet it was only minutes before I ran from the room crying into the arms of my Uncle John, who held me.

Even though I did not understand the meaning of death, as I shed tears I realized that my terrible, terrible wish for my father's death would cause me guilt for many years.

By six-thirty that evening the rows of chairs were all occupied, and there was standing room only as a line of people filed by the casket. As they knelt by my father's coffin, tears flowed, which seemed to bring on a chain reaction from my mother and many others in the room.

At ten o'clock, a musical chime from the large grandfather clock gently signaled that it was time to leave. All the mourners once again went up to the casket, knelt down, then walked over to my mother and kissed her good-night; as each person kissed her, she wept.

When it was our turn to visit the casket, my mother stopped sobbing, and once again kissed my father on the lips. I could hear her say to him, "I will only get to see you for four more days."

On Sunday, it was Father's Day. I bought a small, golden cross for twenty-five cents to pin on my father's lapel, as my last present to him. I also deposited my rosary beads from my First Holy Communion in the coffin with him.

I bent over and whispered, "Happy Father's Day, Daddy."

When my lips touched his forehead, I was shocked by the coldness of his skin.

On the fifth and final day of his public viewing, when we arrived at the funeral parlor for our final goodbye, almost every chair was taken. Seated in the front row with my family, I watched my father's stomach to see if he would take a breath or move in any way. I wondered what I would do if his chest did move.

At nine o'clock in the morning, the grandfather clock chimed to tell us that our final visit was coming to a close. The seven men dressed in black stepped into the room and waited as family and friends made their last farewell. The visitors were ushered out of the room by one of the men in black, and then it was my turn. Quaking and tearful, I whispered into my father's ear that I was sorry for my wish. For the last time, I kissed his forehead and that same cold feeling swept through my body.

Later, the entire funeral procession arrived at St. Athanasius Church. In the sunlight I noticed the casket had a brassy gold tone and the ornaments on the four corners were gold.

From the moment we got out of the limousine, my mother began sobbing. Pallbearers lifted the casket and placed it on their shoulders. As the casket and pallbearers entered the church courtyard, the doors swung open, awaiting the arrival of my father. It was as if God, with his own two hands, had opened the doors. I do not recall the Mass, but I remember the priest circling the casket and the smell of the incense he carried. I also remember that there were wet marks on the casket from the holy water the priest had used to bless the casket as it went into the church.

When the Mass was over, we followed the casket out of the church. We drove toward Long Island, and eventually turned into the gates of Pinelawn Cemetery and drove in until, one by one, all the cars came to a slow stop. We were escorted to the burial site and seated on small white folding chairs. The casket was draped with the American flag. Seven soldiers and a bugler stood in the distance.

The priest began the ceremony. Afterward, there was a seven-gun salute and the bugler played Taps. The American flag was removed from the lid of the casket, folded and presented to my mother. Her tears were uncontrollable at this point. For the final farewell, my mother, Anthony and I were each given a rose, escorted to the casket, and told to place the rose on the lid.

My mother was first, with her brother, John, standing beside her. She lay down her rose, kissed the casket, and was escorted away. When it was my turn, I placed the rose on the casket and said, "Daddy, I'm sorry."

As I looked down, there was a small opening and I could see into the bottom of the grave. Immediately a fear of being placed in the ground and left to be eaten by worms overtook me. I started weeping and was escorted away. As our car pulled away from the grave, I could see my father's casket being lowered into the ground. It would take several years before I realized that many children wish for a parent's death in an innocent expression of anger and that my father's passing after my wish was just an unhappy coincidence.

Later that evening we drove to my grandparents' home. I never again saw the apartment we had lived in before my father's death.

We stayed with my grandparents for about four weeks. By July 15th we moved into a new apartment a few doors away from my grandparents. I did not care about missing my friends. I confined myself to the apartment, except for going to church to pray for forgiveness for the fatal wish that burdened me. When the new school year started, of course, I went to school daily. But at the end of the day, while the other children were outside playing, I stayed inside our apartment.

3. CONNIE'S CALL

A little more than a month after my father's death in the third weekend of July, the phone rang and my nine-year-old sister, Connie, picked it up. I heard her say, "Hello?"

Within seconds she was screaming hysterically, the phone receiver dangling from the wall beside her. My mother and I ran to her and I picked up the receiver to see if someone was on the other end. All I heard was silence.

I replaced the phone on the receiver, while Connie screamed, "Daddy called! Daddy called!"

"You know Daddy's not here any longer," my mother admonished.

"No!" Connie insisted. "Daddy just called and said, 'Hi Connie, this is Daddy. I just arrived; tell Mommy I am waiting at the airport.'"

It was several months before Connie could pick up the telephone after this incident.

As Christmas neared there was talk of our Christmas tree. My mother thought that a Christmas tree was inappropriate yet felt that it was unfair to her children not to decorate for the holiday. We made it through Christmas with a tree and gifts on Christmas morning.

Somehow, the family weathered the period of mourning and we got used to living without a strong male presence. One evening, when I was about fifteen, my mother asked me if I would stay with my sisters while she visited my grandparents. Around nine-thirty, I was sitting on the couch in the living room of our apartment. The windows were open, since it was extremely hot and the kitchen fan did not seem to be stirring up a breeze.

My sisters were asleep in their bedroom located just off the kitchen. I decided that an ice pop would be a cooling treat and I got up to walk toward the refrigerator. There, standing directly in front of me, was the image of my father. He was moving toward my sisters' room. I became so frightened that I was rooted to the floor.

A few seconds later, when I came to my senses and convinced myself that I was just imagining the vision, I ran to my sisters' room to make sure they were both okay. I noticed the air had a strange chill and realized that our dog was barking frantically and backing away from the bedroom door. When I opened the door, the dog edged even further away and kept barking.

In the far end of my sisters' bedroom, their night light glowed dimly. I reached for the switch on the wall and turned on the overhead light. Carol's pillow was on the floor. I walked over to her side of the bed, picked it up and placed it back under her head. The girls were sound asleep.

Everything in the room seemed to be normal except for the strange chill. The pale pink walls almost appeared to be white. The picture of Jesus, a gift from a friend, seemed to give off a comforting warm glow. I looked over toward Connie's side of the bed; she was fast asleep.

As I turned to leave the room I noticed that their closet door was open. Then I knew I had not imagined my father's presence. The flag that had been draped over his casket, folded military style and given to my mother, lay on the floor outside the closet door. It had been tucked away safely on a shelf in the back of the closet.

Leaving my sisters' room I did not realize how upset I was over the flag and the whole incident. Just then my mother returned home and, noticing my strange expression, said, "Ed, what's the matter? What happened?"

With tears running down my face, I told her everything that had taken place. She looked at me in confusion. "Ed, you just imagined this."

"I did not imagine anything," I said. "How did the flag get outside of the closet onto the floor?"

She walked into my sisters' bedroom, and just as I had told her, there was the flag lying on the floor.

"Ed, it must have fallen out of the closet." It was a weak explanation for an event neither of us could explain. After this incident, whenever my father made his presence known to me, the flag somehow appeared.

4 · THE FAN

*B*y the age of fourteen I had become aware of unusual things taking place in my life. Visions of events that would take place in the near future and dreams of things to come became part of my everyday life.

One afternoon I went to have lunch with my grandparents. As I entered the building, I noticed Great-grandma Lily standing at the top of the stairs. This was the second time I had seen her since her passing. An eerie, uneasy feeling came over me, making me feel weak in my knees. As I climbed the stairs I said a silent prayer. At this point, I still had not made the connection with the deeper meaning of my great-grandmother's appearance. It was soon to be made clear.

When I arrived at the top of the landing, I continued up the next flight of stairs to my grandparents' apartment. My grandmother was awaiting my arrival and had lunch prepared.

I never mentioned seeing Great-grandma Lily at the top of the stairs to my grandparents or to anyone else in my family, because the first time I described her visit I had been ignored. After lunch I went home.

That same night, I awoke from a dream so real that I could not shake it. I saw my Uncle Charlie telling silly jokes, as he always did. Suddenly, he grabbed at his chest in pain and fell to the floor. I could see him lying on the floor motionless. I awoke and went into my mother's room and told her about my dream.

"Uncle Charlie died in my dream," I told her.

"It was only a nightmare," she assured me.

Being Italian, in a family that believed in all kinds of superstitions, I had heard somewhere that dreaming of someone's death was actually supposed to mean that person would have a long life. Later that morning, a black bird flew in the kitchen window. Mom did not get upset often, and when she did she usually hid her emotions from us. Yet, when the bird flew into the house, she acted frightened.

After we chased the bird out through an open window, Rose, our neighbor from the floor below, opened the door to see what was happening and I told her about the bird. She did not look at me but directly at my mother and said, "Mary, do you know what that means?"

"No, no. I don't," my mother said sharply. It was almost as if she did not want me to hear Rose's explanation.

In spite of my mother's obvious nervousness, Rose said, "The black bird is a sign that someone's going to die."

My mother looked at me, then back at Rose, and again at me. Just then the phone rang. One of our relatives was on the phone delivering the unhappy news that Uncle Charlie had passed away.

After this incident I became more aware that I had the strange ability to see and hear things that none of my other friends ever spoke of. For example, a few months later my youngest sister, Carol, was invited to go swimming with one of her playmates and her mother. I asked my mom, "Where is Carol? I haven't seen her around."

"She went swimming with Lidia."

Immediately, I pressed her, "Why did you let her go?"

"She has adult supervision," Mom answered.

"She is going to get hurt," I warned my mother.

"Why do you have to say things like that, Ed?"

"Mom, she's going to get hurt," I insisted. No sooner had I expressed my alarm than the doorbell rang. It was one of the other parents coming to tell my mother that Carol had had a minor accident and needed stitches in her head.

Once again, I had been given an insight about something before it happened.

My family, of course, thought it was strange when I forecast the future. Usually they just looked at me and shrugged it off. I did not know that my mother harbored a secret fear of the paranormal, or that many years earlier my father had had a visit from the angelic realm when he was twenty-one. He was told that he would die by his fortieth birthday, and he did, in fact, die at the age of thirty-nine, less than six months from his fortieth birthday.

Within a week of Carol's injury, a bowl filled with gravy and meatballs fell in the kitchen. As I went to help clean the mess, Carol started towards the kitchen. I advised her not to go into the kitchen. She would be hurt and this time it would be more serious than a few stitches.

No sooner had I uttered the warning than Carol, heedless of my prediction, slipped across the kitchen floor and severely cut her hand on the glass from the broken bowl. As she looked down at the three fingers that were hanging by mere threads of skin, she looked at me and said, "You did this!" Then she burst into tears.

Once again Carol was taken to the hospital.

My clairvoyance seemed to be targeted at Carol. The next incident also involved her and broken glass—this time from a door. Once again, she required stitches. On this occasion, when Mom and Carol arrived home from the hospital, we were in the kitchen. I asked Carol, "What happened in the hallway?"

She insisted that she had slipped and her fist had gone through a glass pane. I knew she was not telling the truth.

"Why are you always picking on her?" my mother asked.

"She is not telling you the truth," I answered. "She purposely put her hand through the glass."

As I started to tell my mother exactly what took place, Carol said, "You weren't there, you weren't even home when this happened. How would you know?"

"Why are you making up a story?" my mother demanded of me. "You're lying."

"Mom," I said, "I'm going to prove it to you. I'm not lying, Carol is."

I pointed at the kitchen fan which sat on the window sill. The switch was in the "off" position.

"Mom, do you see the fan in the window?"

"Of course, I see the fan in the window," Mom answered.

"Well, I'm going to turn it on, and that's how I am going to prove to you that I am telling the truth."

"I can go over and turn on the fan, too." Carol said.

"No, I am going to turn on the fan from here," I answered.

I was ten feet from the fan and angry that my mother did not believe me. I pointed my right arm in the direction of the fan switch, and the fan went on.

All of us, including me, stared at the fan in amazement. My mother's first conclusion was that the fan had an on and off thermostat. Then she suggested that the wind was so strong that it turned the fan on.

At that point, Carol became frightened and told me the truth. She had put her fist through the glass.

"Why would you do something like this?" my mother asked her.

"For attention," Carol replied.

I was amazed that the fan had actually turned on. I did not understand how a person's energy could move an object, but deep down I knew that I was capable of it.

To this day I have never attempted to use this type of energy again.

5. "HEAVEN IS LIKE A GARDEN"

*I*n the summer of my sixteenth year, I was without a care. Once again, school was out. My two sisters and my mother were vacationing in Florida for four weeks. Anthony was married and living ten minutes away. I liked the idea of being alone and of taking care of myself.

There was plenty of food, since my grandparents lived just a few doors away. Grandma was an excellent cook, but Grandpa was even better. I spent time shuffling back and forth to their apartment to enjoy great meals and collect my pocket money. On occasion, a friend would stay over.

On Saturday, the third weekend in July, I realized my family would be home from Florida soon and it would take me at least a week to get the apartment back in order. I started gathering the dirty glasses and dishes scattered throughout the apartment and decided on a plan of action. If I cleaned up the kitchen today, and the bathroom the next, and so on, the place would be neatly in order twenty-four hours before they returned.

I started with the dishes, got about halfway through, and took a break to watch TV in the living room. Before I knew it, the afternoon had slipped away. I realized that I had never finished doing the dishes and it was already nighttime. Then, without warning, our dog Mitzie began barking. I started toward her and noticed she was barking at nothing, but was looking intensely in the direction of my sister's room. I opened the bedroom door and, once again, felt a strange chill in the air. I knew this signaled my father's presence.

I quickly decided that before fear overcame me I would investigate the room. I tried to coax Mitzie to go into the room first, but she stopped at the doorway and kept barking.

I got her leash, attached it to her collar, and tried to drag her in, but she kept pulling back and would not go into the bedroom.

I finally succeeded in dragging her into the bedroom with me, and saw that one of the dresser drawers was open. The American flag was lying in it, right on top.

I do not recall taking the dog's leash off, shutting off the lights or locking the door. The ten-minute distance to my brother's house took me less than five. When I arrived I was shaken, and that evening I slept at Anthony's house. However, the next day I was so focused on cleaning up the apartment that I practically forgot about the incident. I decided it would be best to go home, take care of the dog, and get the apartment together. However, I never went back into my sister's room to see if the flag was still there. I did recall that Connie's strange phone call from Father had happened during the third week of July, too.

The next summer, also during the third weekend in July, I once again felt my father's vibration. I hurried to my brother's home, just as I had the previous year. On my way I saw my grandmother on the avenue with some neighborhood women taking fresh air. I told her the story and she suggested that I speak to a priest.

The next day, I went to my parish and asked to speak to a priest. I met with Father Mac. When I told him about my visions and my father's visits from the "other side," he advised me to pray.

"You have to pray," Father Mac told me, "and get those evil thoughts out of your mind. Only God can tell the future. And as far as your visions of your father are concerned, this is where your blood runs cold like a vampire, and it is why you need prayer."

I looked at him in disbelief, but reasoned that he knew more than I did since he was closer to God and had more answers.

"What do you mean about my blood running cold?" I asked. "I don't understand."

"Your thoughts are evil," he replied, "and you must pray."

I was even more confused. Was I evil because I had the ability to communicate with the "other side" and had premonitions? I had not lost my love for God, or for the church, but I was upset and angry with a superstitious priest for calling me evil and comparing me to a vampire. I knew it would take me a long time to remove the sting of his words from my memory.

I've come to believe that people who possess a gift like mine truly carry a cross. There have been many times throughout the years when I believed there was something wrong with me. But each new lesson I learned and each communication from the other side helped me to expand my awareness and granted me the confidence to give those around me comfort and joy.

About two years later, once again during the third week in July, Mom was vacationing in Florida with my sister Carol, while Connie stayed with my Aunt Rosalie on Long Island. I was never fearful of staying home except during this period of time.

It was Saturday, and without mentioning my uneasiness, I asked my girlfriend, Lois, if she would help me clean the apartment before Mom returned home. She agreed to help me. Since it was such a hot day we decided to go to the beach first. After the beach and dinner we returned to clean the apartment. It was not in such bad shape this time. We started in the bedroom, moved on to the living room, dusted the dining room, and finally worked in the kitchen.

I decided I should sweep the hallway stairs while Lois was finishing the kitchen. As I stood in the hallway with the broom, I could hear Mitzie barking. Lois called out to me and I came back into the apartment. She asked me, "Why is the dog barking at your sister's bedroom door?"

At this time in our relationship, I did not wish to share my past experiences with Lois. I thought that if I told her about my clairvoyance she would think that I was out of my mind. But I knew I had to open the door and look in the bedroom. When I opened the door, Lois, who followed me in, asked where the cold air was coming from.

I did not bother to look around for the flag; I knew it would be visible somewhere. Suddenly, the mop flew out of Lois's hands and slammed to the floor. She screamed and said, "I want to go home!"

She claimed that she felt spooked, and of course I had not given her an explanation for the cold air or the mop that moved on its own. Once again, I quickly left the apartment, accompanied by Lois.

I walked her home and continued to Anthony's where I found his wife, Vicki, and told her about my experience at the apartment.

Vicki tried to assure me that I should exert mind over matter and told me I should not worry about strange happenings. While she spoke I could see her looking at my hands curiously. She asked me why my hands were so red. I looked at my hands, then at my feet, and noticed that they were bright red. I remembered that a few days earlier I had prayed for peace of mind, asking God to please give me a sign with my hands and feet so that I would not be afraid of my father's untimely visits. Vicki continued to look at me strangely, and as I explained my prayer, the redness in my skin subsided as quickly as it had appeared.

Later, when Anthony came home, he flung open the door and announced, "I've never felt such an eerie feeling before—I felt like there was someone following me up the stairway."

At this time, Anthony did not know what had taken place at my mother's house, or that I was in his kitchen. That's when I told him about my sister's room and Vicki chimed in about my hands and feet. He described in more detail the sensations he felt in the hallway—a definite coldness that frightened him—then he asked me for Lois's number to verify my story.

Later after dinner, Vicki went to get the sheets for the couch to make my "fright-night" sleeping quarters, and I told my brother that he was sleeping with me.

We took our positions in the living room on the pullout bed. After talking for about fifteen minutes, Anthony said he was really tired and got up to shut off the light. I wanted to ask him to leave the light on, but I did not. I thought if he was giving up his own bed to keep me company, how could I force him to leave the light on?

About ten minutes later, I felt a presence in the room. Anthony was sound asleep. As the presence moved toward me, I was so frightened I couldn't utter a word. The image began to speak, and the voice was familiar. The sound of it was like an angel's harp, soothing every part of my being.

"What do you want from me?" I asked. "You frighten me."

"I truly love you and I am here to say I am sorry," the voice answered. "I didn't mean to frighten you. When I walked on earth there were lessons I had to learn. Again, I did not mean to cause you pain."

"I will listen to all you have to say," I answered. "But you have to make a promise. After tonight you will never come to visit me again, because I'm afraid of you."

I asked a question of the voice before it could reply to my previous statement.

"Is there a heaven?" I asked. "And what is heaven like?"

The reply was, "You should not fear death. It is only a transition, a process that is needed."

"Why?" I asked.

"There are some things I cannot tell you, you will learn them in time."

"But what is heaven?" I persisted.

"Heaven is like a garden of the most beautiful flowers, filled with tranquillity, peace and total love."

"There are things I need to tell you," the voice continued. "Tell your mother that she should start being happy. I am only a breath away. You are truly the head of the household."

"That's not so," I protested. "My brother is older, so that makes him head of the household."

"No, you have the strength to carry many burdens. You may not understand this strength at this moment, but you will. Your sister-in-law carries a child. When your first child comes, he will be named after me."

At this point I was certain I was listening to my father's voice, but I needed to be certain. I asked, "What's your name?"

There was no reply to my question. Instead, he said, "Your sister Carol will go through difficult times. Connie will become like your mother."

I spoke up again. "I am going to get married next year. Will this be a happy, good marriage?"

"This you must learn for yourself. Tell your mother I love her very dearly. Do not become frightened with what I'm about to tell you. One day her worldly possessions will burn."

"Is my mother going to die in a fire?" I asked. "Is this what you're telling me?"

"Do not fear, for no one will be hurt. My time is short and I have to go."

"Why?"

"We are only allowed to spend so much time here," the voice replied.

"Before you go I have to remind you to remember your promise not to come visit me anymore," I said.

"I will not break that promise. I'm only a breath away."

"What shall I call you?"

"As you've always called me. 'Daddy.' "

As the voice said those last words, I was flooded with inner peace. I lost all fear of dying. In fact, I believed that death was not to be feared, but to be embraced. I did not realize that this and all my father's previous visits heralded the beginning of the work I would do someday.

I woke up Anthony and told him everything I had heard.

The next morning, I told Vicki she was going to have a baby.

"I did not think you were nuts last night," she said. "But now I do because I'm not pregnant."

Eight months later the baby was born. It was a little girl, Tiffany. I knew then my firstborn would be a boy and he would be named Philip—after my father.

I did not understand why my father came to me the third weekend of July, since it was not the anniversary of his death. There would be another major event nineteen years later during the month of July, of which I had no inkling at the time.

6. THE RING

We go through life receiving many daily signs. The night before my first wedding I was running errands when someone closed a car door on my left ring finger. If this happened to me today, and there was a marriage taking place tomorrow, I would stop to consider what such a message from the universe meant.

Later, when my wife and I exchanged rings, my ring would not fit because my finger was swollen. Even while I was standing at the altar watching Lois, my wife-to-be, come down the aisle, my inner voice said to me, "You shouldn't marry this girl; this marriage will only last six months. She is only marrying you to get away from her stepfather."

As it turned out, the marriage was one of many painful lessons in my life. Five months after the wedding, I asked Lois if she was seeing someone else. She denied there was anyone else in her life, but a month later she admitted to having an affair with a co-worker during her lunch hour.

We were divorced on May 4, 1969, and that evening I met a petite, beautiful blonde girl, with the most magnificent blue eyes. Her name was Prudence. I took one look at her and told my friend Richie, "You see that girl over there? I'm going to marry her."

"How could you marry her?" he said. You don't even know her."

"Richie, just look at her. She looks like an angel."

We were married on March 1, 1970, and my best man, Richie, was at my side.

Nine months later, on December 22, a special event took place in which I dreamed about my Aunt Frances, who had died of cancer. She appeared to me, looking healthy and happy, yet during the interval of the dream she was engaged in pulling yarn. Long skeins of yarn flowed through her fingers. It seemed as if the strands were never-ending, since she kept pulling and pulling.

The strands were very thick, like a tube, and fastened to the tube was a baby-blue bow. Attached to the end of the tube was a beautiful baby boy.

The next morning my wife's parents and I rushed my pregnant wife to the hospital. We learned from the doctor that there were complications. The baby would have to be birthed by cesarean.

I prayed to Saint Joseph that my wife and child would be safe. Later that evening I went back to visit my wife and discovered that her labor had stopped. It started again much later, about eight-fifteen the next morning, just when I was hit with severe pain in my lower abdomen, as if I had been kicked in the groin. I rushed to the bathroom, trying to expel the pain. When, finally, I was able to release it, I began to sweat. That was when I knew, as I later told my mother-in-law, that Prudence was giving birth.

On our way to the hospital, I remembered my dream about Aunt Frances. I realized that the never-ending roll of yarn she kept pulling with her hands represented my wife's extended labor. And the baby that appeared in the same dream was a dead ringer for my new son, Philip, who was born later that day.

I also remembered with a sense of awe the last visit from my father many years earlier, when he told me that I would have a son and I would name him Philip.

7. THE GREEN TEA ROOM

At the time of Philip's birth, I was working as a buyer in May's department store. There was a stock boy named Carlos, with whom I became friendly. Whenever Carlos decided to get in touch with me, he sent telepathic messages. I did not know what was happening until the day I was on the fifth floor and Carlos was in the basement stockroom. Carlos's name kept popping into my mind, and as much as I tried to concentrate on what I was doing, I could not get his name out of my thoughts. I picked up the telephone and called the stockroom where Carlos answered and said,

"Hi, it's Ed."

When Carlos heard my voice he started laughing. "It works, it works!" he said.

"What works, Carlos?"

"I wanted you to call me," he said. "So I just kept thinking of your name over and over, and here you are."

Carlos's admission led me to confide in him that I had been given power to see into the past and future. I was surprised at my confession, for I seldom spoke to anyone about my clairvoyant abilities.

He said I was indeed gifted, but afraid of what I could not understand. He recommended that I visit a woman in Manhattan at the Green Tea Room, but my first instinct was to ignore his suggestion. Then, he held out his hand, palm up, and asked me to tell him about his life. As I examined his palm, I could hear words flowing from my lips. I could not stop myself from speaking, describing who he was by virtue of a wisdom that came from me like a hidden spring suddenly bursting free.

I had never studied palmistry, but I knew in my inner being that the information I was giving Carlos was accurate. I felt comfortable with the predictions I was making, and Carlos confirmed that everything I told him was true.

He repeated his suggestion that I visit the Green Tea Room. My resistance to the idea came from Prudence. She did not want me to go, insisting that psychics were gypsies and somehow dangerous.

I thought it best not to argue the point. Whether the psychic was a gypsy or not, I was going. I did promise to call Prudence from the city when the reading was finished.

The psychic I met was named Betsy. I was fascinated with her beautiful smile and intense brown eyes.

"Can I help you?" she asked.

"Yes." I said. "I came for a reading."

She looked directly into my eyes and I will never forget what she said.

"Why would you come here for a reading?"

Her question confused me until she added quickly, "Young man, you are highly gifted."

I just stood there staring at her in surprise. "Well, in any case," I insisted, "I would still like a reading."

The statement I remember most from her reading, and which completely changed my attitude toward the unusual things that had happened throughout my life, was: "You hold the keys to the universe. You have a natural gift, or should I say, the gifts of a psychic, telepathic, audio clairvoyant, and psychometric. You were born with these innate abilities." Then, with her eyes burning directly into mine, as if she were trying to pierce my soul, Betsy said, "You have spoken to many people who have passed over."

"What do you mean?" I asked, feeling trapped.

For a moment, she remained silent, slipping into a trance state, then she said, "I am told to ask you, who was the woman in the hallway?"

I had never told anyone outside my family about my sightings of my great-grandmother. Now I found myself explaining those events to a stranger and telling her how frightened I was by them.

"Your great-grandmother was not your only visitor," she said matter-of-factly. "Why did you tell your father not to visit you anymore?"

My eyes welled up with tears. I now trusted Betsy and told her the story of my father's appearances.

"Oh, my dear," she answered, "there will be many visits from many other people's loved ones."

"What do you mean by that?" I asked.

"In time you will understand," Betsy said mysteriously. Then she added, "As I told you when we first started, you hold the keys to the universe. Always remember your insight is a gift from God."

Many of the things Betsy told me that day confused and excited me. But her reading allowed me to understand some of the inexplicable things that had taken place in my life. I tried to contact Betsy many times, but she disappeared, never again to work at the Green Tea Room. It was as if she had vanished from Earth.

8. PHILIP AND FATHER

*F*or the first two years of my marriage to Prudence, we lived at 85th Street in Brooklyn with my wife's parents while an apartment in Park Slope, Brooklyn, was being prepared for us.

Only a week after we moved in with my in-laws, I had a dream in which all of our belongings that were stored in the basement were stolen. I woke up from the dream in the middle of the night tempted to check the basement door.

I decided against the idea since I'd have to wake my father-in-law for the key. What if my dream was a false alarm?

As I was leaving for work the next morning, I decided to check the outside entrance to the basement. The door was ajar as I approached. I could see the basement had been invaded; all our belongings were gone!

The loss of clothing, linens, dishes, was not as upsetting to me as losing the cherished keepsakes I had received from my relatives who had passed over. To me, they were priceless. One missing item was an embossed, gold-lettered plaque on which was printed the Lord's Prayer. It had been given to me by my Aunt Frances's family after she died. The price tag was still on the back, marked only ninety-nine cents, yet this was a treasure that could never be replaced. Another cherished item was my father's belt buckle with the initial "P" inscribed on it. I had hoped to give it to my son one day.

I believed that when things are taken from us, God also sends us rays of love. The person who took the Lord's Prayer must have needed this message. I imagined the thief or thieves would be surprised to discover that they had stolen the words of God. I hoped that they would read this special prayer every day. Maybe it would change their paths in life.

Shortly after this incident, still not trusting my own insights or dreams, I glanced at my mother-in-law's car and noticed the front fender looked dented. I walked over to take a closer look, only to see that it was perfectly fine. There was not a mark anywhere. The vision of the dented fender, however, appeared to me three mornings in a row.

On the fourth morning, I did not even bother to examine the car. As usual, I started up the block to my own car, when a neighbor called out to me, "Did you see your mother-in-law's car?"

I went over to the vehicle and saw at once that the front fender had been damaged during the night.

During the three days when I had had the visions but had verified that the car was fine, I had justifiably thought that my premonition about the stolen property in our basement had just been a dream. But on the fourth day, the smashed fender taught me that the gap of time between a vision and its material manifestation is proof that delays occur between thought and action. Manifestation of a dream can come to full fruition days, weeks, or even months later.

Philip was barely three years old when I overheard him talking to someone in the dining room. As I stepped into the room, I saw that he was facing an empty corner and chattering away to someone who was not there. I did not want to interrupt or startle him, so when he finished giggling and talking, I asked him, "Philip, who are you speaking to?"

"I am talking to Papa," he said.

"No, Philip, Papa's upstairs." I thought Philip was referring to my wife's father, who lived in the apartment above us.

"No, Daddy," he said. "Papa Philip."

My son had never even seen a photograph of my father. The next Sunday we went to visit my mom. I took out a photograph of my father and showed it to my son, and asked who he saw in the photo.

"Daddy," he answered. "That's Papa Philip, who I talk to."

I did not believe that it was right to question him, although I was curious about his conversations. I was afraid that if I questioned him, he would become fearful and possibly close down to the universal messages. I knew then that my young son was able to see the visions that I also saw.

Prudence and I were expecting a new addition to our family. Philip was very excited that he was going to have a baby brother. There was no doubt in his mind, or in mine, that we would have a baby boy. Anthony was born November 8, 1974.

At this time, our lives were going really well. I had just started a new business, a florist wedding center. We had enough money saved for a down payment on a house, and a little left over for a rainy day. Being a Capricorn, I always prepared for rainy days. Philip longed for a yard to play in. He did not like the cement sidewalks of Brooklyn any longer. We started to look for a home in Staten Island. After inspecting several houses, and finding nothing to our liking, once again I had a dream.

I dreamed that I walked into a house with a hallway covered in red paneling. The walls leading up the stairway were covered with the same ugly paneling. I woke from the dream and thought nothing about it. However, within a week we went to look at a home that was lovely on the outside. In fact, from the charming exterior, it seemed to be just what we wanted. Then the realtor opened the door, revealing the ugly red paneling from my dream. Without inspecting any other part of the house, I knew that this was our new home. We moved in in January of 1975 (and quickly changed the wall coverings).

9. SIGNORA MARIA

After moving into our new home, I took a week off from the store. My first day back at work seemed like it was going to be a slow day, so I decided to catch up on some overdue paperwork. However, I was interrupted when my mother called me into the showroom to meet a little old Italian woman. She was very well dressed, with skin as smooth as satin, charcoal eyes, and hair that seemed to be even darker. When she spoke she used broken English with a heavy Italian accent. In one hand she held a walking stick, in the other, a small gift-wrapped box. My mother introduced her as Signora Maria. As I walked over to greet Maria, she handed me the gift.

"This is for your new home," she said.

I had seen Maria come in and out of my store to buy plants and soil. She would take the merchandise, and within a week or two come in and pay for it and take something else. But for some unknown reason I had always kept my distance from her.

"Signora, how do you know about my new home?" I asked.

"I know lotsa things," she replied.

I thanked her for her gift and told her that I would bring it home for my wife to open.

This was my first conversation with Maria and it puzzled me why I was repelled by her. As I turned around to go back to my paperwork, I heard a thumping on the floor. I turned around and there was Maria, who had picked up her walking stick and was thumping it lightly on the floor.

"You will be busy today," she said.

I just smiled at her, then glanced at my mom, shrugged my shoulders, and went back to my paperwork.

It was not more than ten minutes later that the store became so unbearably busy we needed to call in two part-time employees to help out. By early evening, when we had finally slowed down,

I asked my mother if she had told Maria that I had bought a house. She said she had never mentioned it to her.

"Do you think there was a connection with her tapping and us getting so busy today?" I asked her.

I should have realized the response I would get from such a question. I was ignored. The following morning, at a few minutes before ten, Maria came into the store. I smiled at her and she began to tap on the floor.

"Caro mio," she said. "Today you will be busy."

Again, she tapped three times on the floor. Once more, the customers kept us so busy I had to call in the two part-time employees.

We did not see Maria until about a week later when she next came into the store. This time, I was standing in the showroom.

"Hello, signora, what can I do for you?" I asked.

"Buon giorno, caro mio," she said.

At the sound of Maria's voice, my mother came from the back and started speaking Italian, of which I understood very little, with her. Maria was telling my mother that she had been ill for a week and unable to leave her house. Today she was forced to shop because she had nothing in the house to eat.

"Don't you have children that could help you?" my mother asked.

"I was not fortunate to hava children," Maria said. "I hava two step-daughters and they no very nice-a to me."

"If you ever need anything," my mother told Maria, "give us a call and we'll bring it over to you."

This conversation began a weekly ritual for the next several years, because from then on, whenever Maria was ill and needed something, she would call me to bring it to her.

Every time Maria came into the store she would invite us to come to her house for espresso. I always declined her invitation, that is, until April 1975.

One day that April, Maria called the store and said she was not feeling well. She sounded weak on the phone when she asked if I could buy her saltines and milk. I did not hesitate. I said yes immediately, and went to the grocer to buy what she needed, along with a few other grocery items. These I brought to her house. Maria invited me in.

A startling thought occurred to me as I stepped through the door. In fact, my first impression once inside Maria's home was that it was my house.

We went into the kitchen. On the kitchen table were two demi-tasse cups of espresso and a plate of biscuits. She looked into my eyes and she began to tell me about my past, as if she were reading it from a book. It seemed that Maria had been clairvoyant all her life.

Maria spoke about a past life I'd lived in Egypt. She told me that on my fiftieth birthday I would be making what she called "a spiritual journey to Egypt." She mentioned the lisp I had as a child, and the pain it brought to me. She also told me that I should not be afraid of communicating with the "other side." She called these communications my "teachers." Then she proceeded to tell me what would take place in my future.

By this time I had invested in several real estate properties. She prophesied that I would buy a property that was much taller than the other buildings, and this building would bring many difficulties.

Maria was incredibly accurate about my past history, and long after her death her predictions would continue to play out in my future. She told me that my wife was going to have another baby and this time it would be a girl. She also reaffirmed my gift of insight and the lessons I needed to learn. With this gift, the most important lesson I had to learn was to allow the information from beyond to flow, and not to fear the messages I received. Maria explained that if I held back delivering a message from the universe, I would be holding back the person the message was intended for.

"The people willa come to you like you are a magnet," she predicted.

"Maria, I really don't think so," I protested.

"Someday youa will," she smiled.

From that day on, whenever I was able, I visited with my new friend, Signora Maria. We got to know each other very well, in fact, she became like one of the family. By this time I was also call-ing her the Italian Robin Hood. She would call and invite me to come for coffee, and if I was not able to visit with her she would send a tray with a demitasse pot, cups, and biscuits for my mother and me. Her strategy was that I would be forced to return the demitasse set, thus guaranteeing a visit from me that day. If I tried to return the coffee things with one of my staff, she would send the tray and cups back to the store until I returned everything in person.

One day, while returning the tray, I went into her kitchen. As we stood in the kitchen, she asked if I could do her a favor.

"Could you go to the butch?"

"Maria, who is the butch?" I asked.

"The butch," she said again.

"And what do I do at the butch?"

"You buya the meat," she replied.

I started laughing so hard, I could see Maria was becoming angry.

"You laugha at mya English," she fumed. "You say it in Italian."

"Dabutch," I answered.

Buying meat for Maria became my new ritual every week. Maria knew I would never take money. So after our visit, I went to the butcher, ordered meat, and had it delivered to Maria's home. The next day, on my daily visit, I asked her how she enjoyed the meat.

"Caro mio," she sighed. "You know whata happened? My frienda husband leavea her. She crya so hard, I bringa her the meat."

I thought she was teasing me, so I got up and looked in the freezer. It was empty. Of course, I returned to the butcher and placed another order.

It seemed that no matter what Maria asked me to buy for her, she always managed to give it away. It was during the summer when she announced that her washing machine was broken. Little did I know that it had been broken for years, and she did all her laundry by hand. She asked me, "Do you thinka you coulda lend me money and I'll paya you back every week?"

I said, "Maria, what do you need?"

"My washing machine-a, she don't work, she broken."

I found myself in the appliance store buying my little old lady friend a new washing machine. A week later it was delivered to her home.

I was out of town vacationing with my family when the washing machine was delivered. On my return visit I asked Maria how she liked her new appliance. I had discovered that whenever Maria was going to tell me a fib, for some reason she wouldn't use the familiar term of affection, caro mio. Instead she would use my name, adding an "H" so that Ed would sound like "Head."

That was my clue that I was going to hear another Robin Hood story.

"The washing machine-a," she explained. "She didn't work so good, she leaka all over my floor so I sold her."

"Maria, how much did you sell her for?"

"I no sella her, I sella the washing machine-a." With that, she smiled.

"Maria," I said. "You speak English better than I do."

"Head, I give-a you whata I sold her for."

"Maria, I didn't ask you for the money; how much did you sell the washing machine for?"

"You make-a nice-a profit," she said. "Fifty dollars."

"Maria, a washing machine costs close to four hundred dollars, and it's not the money. I bought it for you."

"Caro," she went on. "These-a people so poor."

"Yes, but if you continue doing this, you are going to make me poor," I replied, all the while feeling a twang of love for her generosity in selling the machine to the needy people who couldn't afford one.

"Oh, my caro, youa never be poor," she said as she patted my hand.

I did not consider myself naive, nor did I consider myself foolish, but Maria had a way of getting to my heart, and into my pocket. The washing machine was only one of many items I bought for her without ever receiving payment. Her total income was less than four hundred dollars a month. How could I take money from this wonderful, loving, adorable Robin Hood?

Five years passed and our friendship grew. Maria spent many hours with me and my family. I have never met another person of seventy-seven who had as many friends as she did.

10. THE CRYSTAL BALL

I decided to take the weekend off from the store. My wife thought it would be nice to visit her aunt who lived in Syracuse, New York. We phoned Aunt Annie and made arrangements for our trip. Aunt Annie was excited because she had not met any of our children; she knew them only from photographs.

When we arrived at her old Victorian mansion, I was stunned by the beautiful antiques that graced her home. There was furniture from all over the world: signed original oil paintings, Louis XIV sofas and chairs, lamps, silver, brass, and rare china. An antique dealer would have had a picnic among her treasures. I loved to roam around the house and examine all of these wonderful objects.

Aunt Annie's husband Carl had passed away ten years earlier and much of the furnishings had belonged to his mother and grandmother. Among the collection were letters from Houdini and President Theodore Roosevelt. I also learned that Carl had been known as the most gifted psychic healer of his time. While he was alive he had had two diamonds in his front teeth, which now rested comfortably in a ring on Aunt Annie's finger.

My wife and I slept in the master bedroom with its 1920s wallpaper, high poster bed, and a matching cherry wood and marble-topped dresser. In the far corner of the room was another marble-topped stand holding an oversized antique wash basin.

As we got ready to go to bed, I turned off the lights. A few seconds later the lights switched back on. Again, I turned off the lights, and again they came back on. My wife was frightened, but I just laughed. Earlier in the day, as Aunt Annie and I were sitting on the front porch, she had told me that sometimes she was aware of her husband's presence.

Prudence told me she had to go to the bathroom, but she was not going alone. We got out of bed and she put on her slippers.

We went to the bathroom, then came back to the bedroom. She took off her slippers and left them on her side of the bed. The next morning when she searched for her slippers, they were gone. She made me get up to find them and I discovered that they were now on my side of the bed. Was this Carl's way of making his presence known?

During the night we'd heard footsteps walking back and forth in the attic. Of course, I decided to investigate after breakfast. I climbed the back stairway and was again taken by surprise. Before me stood a life-sized painting of Aunt Annie's husband, Carl Kramer, known for his psychic ability and mystical healing powers. As I looked up at the painting, I was startled, for as I climbed the steps I sensed his eyes burrowing into me. Later, when I asked Aunt Annie about the painting, she explained that it was in the attic stairway because she could no longer bear to have his eyes following her.

I could feel Carl's vibrations within the house, but I did not communicate with him. I was not aware at the time that I could reach into other dimensions to speak with spirits. Instead, I thought that spirits had to contact me.

One day during our visit, I approached the library and slowly opened the doors. Directly in front of me was the carved fireplace, to the right was a large, carved wooden chair. Resting across the arms of the chair was a silk robe, and on top of the robe lay a walking stick. I realized that I had not asked permission to enter this room, so I left the room and closed the door behind me.

Later on that day, I asked Aunt Annie if I could go into the library and look around. Smiling, she told me it would be fine. As I re-entered the library, my eyes went to the chair and I immediately noticed that the silk robe was arranged differently, as was the walking stick. I did not become frightened, but more inquisitive.

To the left of the library was another room. Carl used this room for meditation. In the center of the room was a long wooden table and two chairs. I noticed a magnificent crystal ball in the center of the table along with many other mystical treasures. I could hear my inner voice telling me that all I would have to do was ask, and the crystal ball would be mine. I no longer feared my inner voice, so I decided to ask Aunt Annie. She was happy to give it to me, and the crystal ball became one of my prized possessions. Crystal balls have the ability to reflect visionary patterns and are used by those who are able to perceive other dimensions.

My wife was happy when it was time to say goodbye, while I could have happily stayed another week examining all of the wonderful treasures in Aunt Annie's "museum."

When we arrived home, I worked with the crystal ball until my eyes hurt. After several weeks, I started to use what is called "soft vision." This is the process by which a person looks at the crystal ball gently, lovingly, his eyes fixed slightly above the top of the ball. There is no strain on one's eyes looking at the ball in this manner. One day, the little air bubbles in the crystal globe started to expand, and then, when my focus permitted me to see only the perimeter of the ball, it became milky white. The milkiness cleared, and within I saw a woman holding a walking stick. I could see a date: August 20. I realized that vision in the crystal ball was of my friend, Signora Maria. I was surprised and saddened at the vision, because I knew that another person I loved and cared for would be leaving the earth plane. I put the ball back in its chemise sack. I did not take it out for several years, because after that vision of Maria I could feel fear stir in my stomach. I thought back to my conversation with Father Mac many years before and his foolish, superstitious words, "Your blood runs cold like a vampire."

I was still not ready for the gift of sight.

11. MARIA'S PASSING

*M*aria was hospitalized in the last weeks of her life, and only my wife and I were allowed at her bedside. She was so ill and spent so much time in the hospital that she was no longer concerned with her friends' troubles. She stopped asking me to go to the "butch" and dropped her antics to help her needy friends. Sadly, when her generosity ended, all the people around her withdrew.

The night before Maria's passing, my father-in-law was in the same hospital and my wife and I went to visit him. I asked my wife if we could shorten the visit with her father so that we could also pay a call on Maria.

I remembered my vision of Maria, the one I'd seen in the crystal ball that included the date, August 20. It was now August 19. Even though I was afraid to trust that vision, I knew that Maria's time was short.

I had told my wife that Maria was not doing well, but I had not given her any details about her condition. When we entered her room in the intensive care unit, Prudence looked at me as if I had lied to her about Maria's condition. We were surprised to find Maria sitting up in bed, looking well, chatting away with the nurses. She greeted my wife and me lovingly.

During our conversation she asked me for one last favor, "Caro mio," she chuckled. "He's-a like-a my boyfriend," she explained to my wife. I knew better than to ask her what she was plotting. She waited a few minutes and then looked into my eyes.

"I musta tella you these things so you are prepared," she began, "In the red box, where my tarot cards are, is my will. There is one-a thing I can't give-a away—my funeral. In exchange for my funeral, I leave-a you my house. Mya home was yours from the firsta day I meta you. Even if youa had no done-a alla those wonderful thingsa for me. Youa do not have to spenda too much money. I have a plot, and I woulda like to be buried with mya husband, Roberto.

"There'll only be eleven people at my funeral," she continued. "And after I'ma with Roberto, most of thesa people will come-a and tella you that I promised them mya personal things. You don't give-a anything to anyone. When I close-a my eyes, you aska my boarder to leave."

"Maria, don't talk like this," I begged.

"Justa remember everything's I have-a said," she replied. "There isa something very special that I wanted to give-a to you for the longest time. Looka for the black velvet bag, there are gold coins ina the bag, Roberto gave-a them to me as gifts. This is the only money I have."

"Maria, I do not care about the money, or the house," I protested.

She interrupted. "Caro, only one-a more thing, and it's not too mucha money. I was paying Mr. Gordon five-a dollars a week for mya wristwatch. I still owe him twenty-five-a dollars. And youa know Mr. Campo, ina the gift store. He is honest, he will tell youa exactly how mucha I owe him. I don't owe any money to anyone else."

I was sad when visiting hours were over and we were forced to say goodbye to our friend.

"Maria, don't worry about anything," I assured her. "Everything will be fine."

She grasped my hands firmly, as if she really did not want to let go. I explained to her that I was unable to visit her the next afternoon, but would return in the evening.

The following day there were many demands at the store that required my attention. At five-thirty I was in the rear of the store when I smelled a familiar odor: the distinctive scent of the intensive care unit. Then the air grew cold. I called one of my employees, Irene, to come to where I stood and asked her what she smelled.

"Disinfectant . . . like in a hospital," she replied.

"Maria came to say goodbye," I said.

I frantically called the hospital and asked about Maria's condition. The switchboard operator reported that she was resting comfortably.

I called back repeatedly within the next fifteen minutes and, filled with dread, asked the same question. I received the same reply, but with each phone call the switchboard operator was becoming more and more irritated. I asked Irene to place a call and she, too, heard the same reply: "Resting comfortably."

Finally, I dialed the hospital one last time. I apologized for my persistence and explained that I was bringing an elderly friend with me to the hospital, and that she had a very bad heart.

"When I knock on the door, the nurse is going to tell me that Maria has passed away, and she will ask why I was not notified," I predicted. I hoped that by explaining my premonition that the operator would cooperate.

"I told you that she was resting comfortably," she snapped. "It's probably your imagination."

With that she disconnected the line and the phone went silent.

I picked up Bella, Maria's friend, without mentioning my premonition, and we drove to the hospital. Arriving at the front door, we entered and hurried to the intensive care unit. Just as I had predicted, the nurse met us at the door and asked, "Weren't you phoned?"

"No. Why?" I replied.

"Maria passed away at five-thirty."

After I helped Bella recover from the shock of the sad news, I looked for the switchboard operator, ready to give her a piece of my mind.

"How did you know that Maria had passed away?" the operator asked. "I tried to call you, but you had already left. My condolences to you, but how did you know before I did?"

I looked at her without speaking, my eyes filled with tears, and walked away.

After taking Bella home, I returned to the store and called Prudence to tell her about Maria's death. Then I placed a call to the funeral director, Michael DeLuca, to make the funeral arrangements. He explained that, since I was not a relative, I needed permission from Maria's will to make funeral arrangements. I walked the block to Maria's home. Although she had given me keys earlier, I felt uneasy entering her home knowing she was no longer there. I rang the bell and her boarder came to the door.

I explained that Maria had passed away and that I needed to get something from the kitchen. The kitchen felt empty without Maria's familiar presence. I picked up her red makeup case and placed it on the table. My heart pounding, I pushed the button to open the case, but it would not budge. I tried several times and still it would not open. I made a final attempt, and it seemed as if the lid flew open in my hands.

I emptied the contents, including her tarot cards and religious paraphernalia. At the bottom I found her will, the deed to the cemetery plot, and the bill from her husband's funeral. I removed all the papers I needed, and with great care replaced the rest of the contents into the case.

Just as Maria predicted, eleven people attended her wake and she now rests next to her beloved Roberto. In my grief, I let my heart take over and did not listen to my dear friend. I allowed her boarder to stay on for another month instead of immediately asking him to leave. I never found the black velvet bag containing the gold coins. All of Maria's furnishings, clothing and personal belongings were given to needy people. I believe in my heart that Maria would have wanted it that way.

I knew that somehow Maria was fully aware that all the wonderful things she had predicted for me would come true. I remembered the day we sat in her living room and she waved her hand and started to speak in Italian.

"Maria, you know I don't understand Italian," I interrupted.

"Oh, sorry, caro," she replied. "Your wife is going to have another baby."

"I do not think so, Maria," I said. "Not now."

"And it's a girl," she pronounced.

This turned out to be one of Maria's most precious predictions. Our daughter, Michelle, was born within one year of Maria's words, on March 6, 1977.

A short time after Maria's passing, some of her clients came to my store and asked me if I would perform a reading for them. One woman I remember very clearly. I asked her why she came to see me, since Maria was really the psychic.

"Maria told me a long time ago that you were a very gifted reader," she answered.

I believe that not only did Maria leave me her worldly belongings, but she also opened the door to my understanding and opened me more fully to the universal messages I was receiving.

My only communication with Maria after her passing occurred in a dream. In it, Maria told me that she likes her house as it was and wanted me not to change it. A few days earlier I'd contemplated buying a larger headstone for Maria and her husband. After Maria's message via the dream, I decided to leave the original headstone as it was.

12. GAINING INSIGHT

*I*t would seem that having insight or the ability to see the future would ease life's hard lessons and bring exciting rewards. Unfortunately, this is not always true. In my experience, although I can see into the future I cannot always detach myself emotionally enough to be objective or act on my perceptions.

In January 1978, I felt suicidal for the first time in my life. At the time I was coping with a serious stomach ailment. My doctor ordered extensive testing and told me that there was a possibility that the tests would detect cancer. I dreaded putting my wife and children through a slow, agonizing illness and I became more and more distraught.

One night before bed, I knelt down and prayed that the angel of death would visit me. I knew I could not commit suicide by my own hand, but when I prayed for the angel of death I realized it was a form of "mental" suicide. The same night I woke up feeling a presence in the room. As I opened my eyes, there by the side of my bed stood a very tall figure. It put out its hand and, having no fear, I placed my hand in his.

"I come to answer your prayer," the voice murmured. Next I felt myself lifted from the bed. It was at that moment, as I floated above my sleeping wife, that I realized I was not ready to die. Panicked, I struggled to free myself from my visitor's grip. However, the mysterious figure still loomed before me.

"I am not ready to go," I said. "I don't want my family to watch me suffer."

The voice spoke, vibrating with love: "You have so much work on Earth to do. Clear your mind of any disease."

My movements rocked the bed, waking my wife. Startled, she yelled, "Why are you bouncing all over the place?"

"You're worried about me bouncing and they're coming to take me!" I yelled back to her.

"Ed, you're just having a nightmare," she said. "Just go back to sleep."

A few weeks after this incident I received the results of my medical tests. I was overjoyed that the angel of death was not going to take me yet, because the tests showed a small benign growth, but no real threat to my life.

This was a turning point for me. I became more sensitive to people's needs. I began giving readings using tarot cards and interpreting the information in the palms of my clients. Instead of asking for a fee in return for a reading, I requested that they say a prayer as their payment. Sometimes I met people who were contemplating suicide, and because of my own experience I could work closely with them. It is my practice to never ask people if they are considering suicide. Instead, I gently probe to determine whether they are struggling with thoughts about remaining on the Earth plane. Then I remind them of all the wonderful things in their lives, and of all the people who love them. I know that they have the right to feel their pain, but I try to convince them to find a way to learn from their experience.

For example, a young man came to see me whose calm words were quite different from the vibrations I was receiving. We discussed his father's passing and how difficult it was for him, because his finances changed after his father's death. It seemed that no matter how hard he tried, he became mired deeper and deeper in debt. I asked him if his financial problems were the reason he was struggling with the question of whether or not to remain on the Earth plane. His eyes brimmed with tears as he asked me what I meant. I knew he understood me, so I asked him if he was suicidal. He broke down weeping, and told me that suicide was the only way out of his problems. I asked him if he had ever considered his mother's feelings, and he admitted he hadn't. After he calmed down, I instructed him to close his eyes and take in a series of long, deep breaths.

Next I asked him to imagine his mother's face and how she would feel when she found his lifeless body. He sobbed harder. Once again, when he was calm I asked him to do the breathing exercise and to summon a vision of himself two years in the future. I asked him to look ahead at his financial situation and he told me he saw himself no longer in debt. I asked him to breathe in his vision of no more money troubles and told him that he was capable of manifesting whatever he needed. I still occasionally see my client and he is extremely successful.

I do a lot of thinking as I commute from Staten Island to Brooklyn each day. One winter morning, as I drove toward my store, I mulled over the dream I remembered from the previous night. I could not understand the meaning of the dream and it puzzled me. In it I saw a young man of about nineteen with his arms raised. I recognized him as John, the son of two of my friends. He held a gun in his right hand, and I heard his words, "This is my surprise, and I want a bow on my casket."

I had awakened from the dream at two o'clock in the morning, wondering why I was dreaming about John. I also wondered if I should call his parents and tell them about my dream. John's parents, Linda and Ed, owned a variety store across the street from my business. Unfortunately, I never made the phone call. When I arrived at the store I discovered John had died from a gunshot wound. I was angry with myself because I thought that if I had called his parents when I awoke, maybe I could have somehow prevented their son's untimely death.

This was a very important lesson for me. I learned to act on the warnings and symbols that appear in my dreams.

There were times I thought that God was cruel to allow these tragedies. Children were born blind and crippled, and I was often unable to help people cope with their pain. What I have since learned is that God has given us free will, and we must think for ourselves, make our own decisions, and take responsibility for them. Everything we do creates a ripple effect that eventually returns with the same energy. All our actions—good or bad—always come back to us.

It would be less than two months after John's death that I had another nocturnal visitor. Walking through the house, I saw a shadow in the doorway of my bedroom. Someone had come to say goodbye. However, as soon as I spotted the fleeting shadow it disappeared. The next morning while driving to the store, I passed a catering business and realized that the owner was my late-night visitor. I pictured the owner, Jim, and realized he was the man in my vision.

Everyone considered Jim a tough guy. All Jim's employees jumped to attention when he entered a room. That day I discovered that he truly was an imposing character—even after his death. I was alone in my store when a man entered with his hand in his pocket acting as if he had a gun. He told me he was going to rob me, and he demanded that I give him whatever cash I had on hand. As the robber finished his threat, Jim happened to walk into the store. He seemed to instantly understand what was taking place and threatened the would-be thief, warned him that he was going to split his head open, and ordered him to leave. I never saw anybody run so fast. Jim laughed as if he had just won a long shot.

Looking at Jim, I had the eerie feeling he was a spirit rather than a flesh-and-blood person, and my instincts were correct. Jim had already passed away. His death had occurred the night before, probably not long before he visited me in my bedroom to say goodbye.

A few weeks after Jim's funeral I had another visit from him, and he asked me to help his family. He told me there was a lot of confusion since his death, and his family was not adjusting well. I called Jim's daughter, Stephanie, and told her about her father's message. She asked me if I would come to her home.

When I arrived I rang the doorbell. There was no answer. I went back to my car to wait for her. As I looked back toward the house, I was shocked to witness a fire starting inside. I ran from my car, hurried to the house and peered through the window. There was no fire. Just then Stephanie arrived and I told her what I had seen. "Boy, don't you have an active imagination," she laughed. She wanted to know if I felt her father's presence in her home. When I told her that I sensed her father nearby, she spoke again.

"Not only do I feel my father's presence," Stephanie said. "but I smell his cologne."

The reason Stephanie had called me, I discovered, was to ask for my assistance in locating an article belonging to her father. I gave her detailed information about the missing article and later discovered the information I gave was correct. We discussed her mother's distress and I warned Stephanie that she needed to watch her mother closely. Then the next day, Stephanie called me to tell me that a fire started in her kitchen shortly after I left.

It was only a month after speaking with Stephanie that she called me to tell me that her mother wanted to commit suicide. She was beside herself with worry, and begged me to please help her. For the next two years, I worked in person as well as on the telephone guiding Stephanie's mother through her pain.

Often my family visited me at my store. On one occasion on a busy Saturday, the day before Easter 1980, my uncle John and Aunt May were visiting with my grandparents for the holiday. Since they were not staying over for Easter Sunday, they dropped by the store to say hello to my mother.

In an Italian family there were always lots of hugs and kisses when we greeted each other. When I hugged my Uncle John, I placed my hands on his back and sensed a massive, white, jelly-like substance under his skin. I did not mention my discovery to my aunt and uncle. But I believed that I needed to share my concerns with my mother. After mulling it over for several hours, I finally told Mom that I needed to speak to her.

"Mom," I began. "I don't want to say anything that's going to hurt you. But Uncle John has lung cancer."

Her eyes immediately welled up with tears.

"Why? Did Aunt May tell you that?" she asked. "Or did my brother?"

"No, Mom, I could feel it in my hands."

By this time my mother knew better than to shrug off my intuition. I warned her only because I thought it best she knew.

"Ed, what do you think the outcome will be?" she asked.

"Uncle John is going to have lung surgery," I assured her. "He's certainly not ready to die."

Not long after Easter, Uncle John had a lung removed, then began chemotherapy. When the family learned that Uncle John needed surgery, my mother prepared herself for the worst, although she was slightly confident in my prediction. The surgery went well. Five years later, Uncle John's health suddenly began slipping again. On that day, he made a strange statement which none of his family understood: "Thirteen pink stones."

On the morning of May 13, I received a phone call telling me that he was failing. I went to pick up my cousin Linda and we drove together to the hospital in New Jersey. About fifteen minutes into the drive I told Linda that I hoped I was wrong, but I sensed that Uncle John had just passed away. When we arrived at the hospital, we were ushered to a waiting room, then the head nurse told us that Uncle John had died an hour earlier.

His funeral was very sad. Watching my grandparents say goodbye to their son was hard for all of us. As we arrived at his graveside, I noticed the mausoleum was made of pink marble. I realized what my uncle had meant thirteen days earlier when he said, "Thirteen pink stones." He was pronouncing his own death date, the thirteenth, and describing the opening to his crypt which was made of pink marble.

After Uncle John's funeral service, family and friends gathered at my aunt's home. By this time it was common knowledge among my cousins and some of my older family members that I was able to see into the future as well as the past.

My cousin Charlie must have mentioned this to his friend Buddy, because Buddy took me aside and asked me if I would mind telling him something about his future. I asked Buddy for permission to place my fingers in the center of his palm. I went on to explain that this touch connected me with his vibration. For me, this spot acts like a conduit, and putting my fingers there is like putting an electrical plug into an outlet so that the current travels in a full cycle.

Buddy held out his hand and I began the reading. As I was

given information, I asked him if he preferred that the reading be held in private. He assured me that he had nothing to hide. I did not want to cause him any pain. I asked again if he was certain he wanted to hear what I had to say, and he replied affirmatively.

I started to describe a letter he had recently received. I described how he could not stop crying when he opened the letter.

Buddy looked in amazement. "What does the letter say?' he asked.

"It is about your disease," I answered.

"Ed, you are absolutely correct," he said. "Will my life be short?"

I felt no need to tell him when his life would be over. Instead, I replied, "Life is never short, it only seems so when we look ahead and don't enjoy the moments of today. Trust in God."

I didn't see Buddy again until two days before he passed away, when again I had a premonition. I called my Aunt Carol. "Charlie's friend Buddy will pass away soon. Your son needs you," I told her.

Later that day my aunt arrived at Charles's home. Buddy passed away two days later.

13. FAITH

*B*y April of 1984 I was having strong visions once again that I would lose someone I loved very dearly. The visions were of my mother and they were letting me know that she would be leaving on April 3, 1987. I didn't tell her about my visions. Concerned, I kept asking her if she would go to the doctor for a checkup, but she insisted that there was nothing wrong with her. For the next months, as the thought of losing her became stronger, I tried to push the thought from my mind and replace it with a prayer.

Two months later, in June, my mother had to be rushed to the Lutheran Medical Center. After extensive testing, her doctor informed us that there was a tumor lodged in the bronchial tube in her lung, and the only way they could stop its growth was with radiation treatment. If she did not receive immediate treatment, they warned, she would only have three days to live.

As her treatment began, we learned how strong she really was, and her strength gave us the courage to hold on to our faith.

As the hours of the next three days crawled past, I felt like a prisoner awaiting the electric chair. Every moment felt like hours. I was grateful when the three days were over and my mother was still alive, but the following days were just as draining.

Finally, we received word from the doctor that he wanted to speak with us. He reassured us that the tumor had started to shrink. We were truly elated by the news. Unfortunately, there was a catch—the kind of cancer that plagued my mother would have to be monitored very carefully. It could come back. If there were signs of the slightest bit of pain in any part of her body, she would have to be examined immediately. According to the doctor, her type of cancer showed no mercy, engulfing the entire body like a piranha attack.

As her treatments progressed, I noticed changes in my mother;

her sweet-sounding voice took on a gravelly tone. Yet through it all she never complained. In fact, she steadfastly assured me that she would be fine.

We were overjoyed when she was released from the hospital five weeks later. My sister Connie took Mom into her own home to care for her, and made arrangements to transport her to the hospital for continued radiation treatments. As the weeks went by, Mom's treatments became a normal part of our lives.

By the new year of 1985, Mom seemed to be back to normal and the treatments were long over. The only reminder of her ordeal was the change in her voice. God was truly on my mother's side as her health remained stable until October of 1986, when she began her second battle with cancer.

We knew after the first radiation treatments that she was not a candidate for more radiology. We were told that her lungs were like tissue paper and that half of one lung needed to be removed. The surgery was scheduled for nine a.m.

The day of the surgery, Connie and I went to the hospital. When we arrived, the nurse told us our mother had already been wheeled into surgery. Remaining calm during a crisis is not one of my strengths. As we waited for Dr. Connelly to report the outcome of my mother's lung surgery, my brother, Anthony, talked to me, but so intense was my concentration on my mom's outcome that his words passed over my head. My eyes were glued to the shiny elevator doors, where I expected to see the doctor appear. The doors seemed to draw me like a magnet, for I was unable to focus on anything else. Each time they slid open, my mind raced with anticipation.

My life had been filled with visions and premonitions, both wonderful and sad. Yet on this day, as my mother lay ill, I did not want to know if God had made his final decision to reach out and call her home. It was in this frame of mind, with my eyes closed, that I heard a familiar voice from the past, a voice from childhood that I thought I had long forgotten.

"It is not her time," the voice whispered. "Look within yourself, and you will know the answer."

When my mother's operation was over, Dr. Connelly came to tell us that he believed the surgery was successful. Yet as I looked at the doctor, in my heart I knew he was not telling us the whole truth.

On my way home, I thought about how much paperwork waited for me at the store. I'd have to finish it before I could return to the hospital during visiting hours to see Mom when she was awake and recovering. There was bookkeeping to be done and checks to be written, so I quickly planned my day in my head.

I left the house early the next morning to accomplish all the chores at the store. I sat down with the checkbook to pay bills, and on the first check I wrote I discovered I had post-dated the check about six months. I had written April 3, 1987. Was this another way for the universe to give me confirmation of my previous vision, that my mother would leave us on that date?

I finished my tasks at the store and left for Sloan-Kettering Hospital. Mom looked drained and exhausted. It was apparent that she was still in a lot of pain. I kissed her hello and she told me that her doctor had informed her that her surgery had gone well.

"Now, I want to know what you think," she said.

"Mom, Dr. Connelly said everything went well. That's exactly what he told us."

"I am not talking about what the doctor had to say," she insisted. "I want to know what you have to say."

"Mom, I have nothing different to say than what the doctor told you."

"Are you sure?"

"Mom, you'll be out of the hospital soon enough."

"I need to be home to take care of Prudence," she said, referring to our daughter who is named after my wife.

"Mom, you'll be taking care of Prudence for as long as necessary."

The expression on my mother's face told me she knew I was not telling the truth. When she was finally released from the hospital, she returned quickly to her normal affairs, making plans with her granddaughter and venturing on outings with her friends. Mom cherished her independence, preferring to drive herself and not rely on others to chauffeur her. She was also spending one day a week in the store answering the telephone.

As I promised, Mom traveled to Florida with little Prudence at the end of the school year. Before the trip she had a checkup at Sloan-Kettering and was given a clean bill of health. The examination revealed that there wasn't a trace of cancer in her lungs. An appointment was made for a subsequent exam in early December.

As Christmas grew closer, Mom was busy doing her holiday shopping and decorating her house. It was her favorite time of year. As Mom and Connie sat in Dr. Richard's office conferring over details, he suggested that she be admitted to Sloan-Kettering for the new tests. Mom refused, informing him that Christmas was only two weeks away. She promised the doctor that she would enter the hospital for tests right after the new year.

When Christmas Eve came, my home was completely decorated for the festive holiday. The ten-foot tree was a dazzling array of decorations and lights, garlands graced the stairway, poinsettia stood by the fireplace, and all the Christmas stockings hung on the mantel.

As I think back to that Christmas Eve, I realize that my mother needed to express her emotions as all of us gathered. Yet Mom must have realized that we were all fighting our fears and hiding our tears. Mom proudly announced that the gift she brought was for both Prudence and myself. My wife understood that I should open this final Christmas gift from my mother. With my wife's kind assistance, I unwrapped and opened the package. I reached in and carefully took out tissue-wrapped bundles. The first figure was the Blessed Mother, and then I unwrapped a complete nativity scene. As I held the small figurine of Mary in my hand, I turned it over. It was inscribed, "Christmas 1986, Mom." As hard as we tried, none of us could hold back the tears.

As I knelt down to hug my mother, I told her how much I loved her and how much I would cherish her thoughtful gift, handcrafted with tenderness and love. "Mom, we're only crying out of joy," I assured her. "You're going to be perfectly fine."

Once again she looked directly in my eyes and said, "Only you know if that's true."

I could see that she was searching my face for the truth. Looking back, I realize that it was wise at the beginning of the evening to allow our emotions to flow. With them released, it was easier to laugh and enjoy our holiday together. During the festive Christmas dinner we served all of Mom's Italian favorites: lobster oregano, crabs in red sauce, shrimp scampi, mussels in light red sauce, and *frutte di mare,* fruit of the sea, an assorted fish salad.

A week later, we all watched Dick Clark's New Year's celebration on TV until the ball dropped at Times Square. At the stroke of midnight, we also heard the neighborhood church bells ring. There were tears for husbands, fathers and brothers who had walked into God's light. My own tears wet my eyes, for I knew that the end of my mother's time was "just a breath away." We all hugged and kissed and expressed our love for one another. Later, as my mother drove away, I watched the car make a left turn at the corner. I knew that it would be the last time she would spend the holidays with us.

Thursday, the day Mom was scheduled to begin her tests, came too quickly. I arrived at her home at nine in the morning to drive her to the hospital. When we arrived and Mom walked through the doors, I could actually see her energy shift. I immediately knew that she would never leave the hospital walking on her own two feet.

When I visited her on January 17, she wished me "happy birthday" and handed me a card and a small box wrapped in gold foil paper.

"I wanted to give you something special for your fortieth birthday," she said.

Again, I tried to hide my emotions. I truly wanted to believe what the doctor had told me earlier that day, that Mom was going to be fine. He had explained that she was going to be fitted with a back brace which would relieve the pressure on her sciatic nerve. He also said that she would be released from the hospital as soon as the brace arrived.

"Mom, I received a wonderful birthday present from the doctor today. After you get the back brace, you're going home."

She just looked at me, nodding in seeming agreement, but there was no smile. She insisted I open the box.

The box contained a disk made of black onyx imprinted with the face of Christ.

"I wanted you to have something very special for this birthday," she explained.

When visiting hours were over, Mom insisted that I leave, but I protested.

"I always stay until the guard comes and says I have to leave," I said.

"Well, tonight I'm a little tired," she answered. "I want to get some sleep. So you leave now and I'll see you tomorrow."

Reluctantly, I left, convinced in my heart that my mother had conspired with her doctor to have him tell me that everything was fine in order to make my fortieth birthday free of worries.

For Valentine's Day we sent Mom a dozen roses along with a three-foot, heart-shaped balloon which was tied to the end of her hospital bed. That month our conversations suddenly took a different turn. She called me at work one day and said she needed to see me. When I arrived at the hospital, I knew from my mother's questions that she had wholly accepted the unusual gift that God had given me.

In a bedside scene described in the Introduction of this book, she turned to me and said, "Tell me how to die. I've never done this before." We spent the afternoon talking about life after death, our belief in the ability of spirits to visit us and watch over us, and other spiritual subjects. Shortly after this conversation, Mom revealed that she also had the gift of seeing into "the other side."

One day while I was visiting her, she asked me to draw the drape that hung between her bed and the bed of the woman next to her.

"Mom, why are we closing the drape?" I asked.

When the drapes were closed to her satisfaction, she nodded toward her roommate's bed and whispered, "I don't want to mix her company with mine."

I was certain that the woman in the next bed was alone. Yet to be certain, I peeked outside the drape.

"Mom, the lady is by herself, there's no one there."

However, Mom insisted that there was someone there.

"Okay, if there is somebody there," I challenged, "what does he look like?"

She described a man, about five feet tall, with a pencil-thin mustache. She also added that her roommate had a blood disorder and that the man was waiting patiently for her to accompany him. At times, my psychic knowing was overwhelmed by emotion, but I just let my mother go on with her story and hoped that her reasserted cancer had not spread to her brain. Later, when the children of the woman in the next bed arrived to visit, I waited for the opportunity to speak to her son alone. As soon as he left the room, I followed and struggled with how to broach the subject.

"I believe my mother recognizes your mother from the neighborhood," I said.

Then I described the gentleman my mother claimed she had seen in the room.

"That was my father," the son replied. "He died twenty years ago."

I simply stared at him, yet I still needed to confirm Mom's information about his mother's illness.

"Will your mother be going home soon?" I asked. He answered, "I hope so, but my mother has leukemia."

Within three days the woman passed over, reunited with—according to my mother—her beloved husband.

14. MY MOTHER, MY TEACHER

*I*n early March, Mom's lungs were x-rayed. When I arrived at the hospital to visit, she told me that the x-ray film clearly showed deterioration in her right lung and the spread of cancer to her left lung. Then she said that, although she could live for a long time, her choice was to die.

"Mom, who told you this?" I asked.

She just looked at me without answering. I asked again, but she did not answer. I excused myself, telling her that I was going to the cafeteria, but I really intended to speak to the doctor.

In his office, I saw kindness in his face, but I was angry that he would share the x-ray results with my mother before consulting her family. Previously, I had been emphatic that she not be told how serious her illness was. He patiently listened as I berated him for informing my mother without our permission.

Gently, he said, "I'm sorry, but I haven't told your mother anything. The results of the x-rays aren't in yet. They won't be for a few hours."

I asked if he was sure, and if it was possible that someone else could have shown her the x-ray report.

He assured me that the results would be delivered directly to him, then he would discuss them with Dr. Tricarico, and finally with me. Baffled, I repeated what my mother had told me and asked again if he was certain that no one had revealed any information to her.

He shook his head and said, "Absolutely not."

I was still beside myself over Mom's news and questioned her when I returned to her room. I asked how she had obtained the information. She assured me that the results hadn't come from her doctor.

"If he didn't tell you, who did?"

She hesitated for a moment, then looked directly into my eyes.

You would think that after all my psychic experiences I would have been prepared for her answer: "Your father and my brother John."

"How did Daddy get in the room?" I questioned. "Through the door?"

With a child-like gesture, she pointed toward the ceiling. "There, there is the door," she explained.

"Mom, what door?" I asked, bewildered.

"There is a door, and your father and Uncle John came through. I have been telling you to move that big balloon because it blocks the view," she said.

"Mom," I went on, "is that why you are always looking up at the ceiling?"

"Yes," she replied. "Now, will you remove the balloon? It's not that I don't love the present, but I have to look into the doorway."

Several hours later I was called into the hallway by both doctors. They confirmed the x-ray results exactly as my mother had described them.

"I don't know how your mother got the results before I did," her doctor said, clearly baffled.

Once again, my mother, my teacher, confirmed for me that other dimensions are a reality.

When no one was around, Mom would ask me to tell her the story of the light after death, which I had described to her earlier. She wanted to make certain that she would not forget anything, so I repeated what I had told her. One day, she said to me, "When my time is near, I wish for no one to be in the room. If any of you are present, my love for you will stop me from going."

As the month of March drew to a close, I knew in my heart that Mother's time was drawing near. However, her doctors insisted that she would live for quite some time and were deciding whether to move her to the terminally ill ward. They suggested that later we should place her in a hospice. During this period I was part-owner of a bridal salon. In the last week of March, my partner, Mike, brought in a yard of pale blue French silk embossed with teardrops of deep blue and silver. I asked him to order ten yards of the fabric for me. I met with Lillian, a seamstress, and we designed my mother's farewell dress. Lillian asked me if I wanted to see the dress when it was completed. I said that the only time I wanted to see the dress was when my mother was wearing it.

"How much time do I have to make this dress?"

"Not very much time at all."

When I arrived at the hospital that day, I spotted my brother and sister, Anthony and Connie, in the cafeteria, and told them about the dress. Surprisingly, they took my news well. "Do you think Mom's time is soon?" Anthony asked.

I nodded yes. I explained that she had made plans for all the details of her funeral attire including her hair, makeup and nail polish, right down to her undergarments. My mother was determined to leave Earth with dignity. She had even chosen a funeral home. While it was difficult to listen to my mother plan these intimate arrangements, I was grateful and relieved that she had made her own decisions.

As I repeated our conversation, Anthony and Connie both seemed surprised that she would have such a conversation with me. At the time none of us realized that she was guiding me toward the work I do today. I had always doubted whether I was truly capable of communicating with those who had passed over, despite happenings that demonstrated the reappearance of those who had died. Now, I was witnessing my mother's conversations with the other side, and ultimately this fact encouraged me to work with my gift.

After our talk, we went upstairs to visit our mother and she took her usual single sip from her favorite strawberry malted. Mom asked Anthony and Connie to leave her alone with me for a minute, so that we could speak privately.

"When will my dress be complete?" she asked.

"Mom, what dress?"

"The dress you're having made for me, the blue one."

"Mom, I don't know what you're talking about."

While I felt uneasy about lying to Mom, I still couldn't summon the courage to tell her about the dress.

"When it's finished, I want to see it," she instructed. "And if you can't bring me the dress, bring me a piece of the fabric."

"Mom, there is no dress," I insisted.

"Yes there is. You just finished telling your brother and sister about it."

"How do you know what we discussed? We were five floors below you."

Once again, she pointed upward to that invisible doorway and said, "Your father."

When I left her that evening, she reminded me to bring her a piece of the silk fabric.

On the fourth floor of the hospital, Mrs. LaGravanece, the mother of one of my employees, lay ill. She had been hospitalized for about two weeks, then passed away during the night. When I reached the hospital on the following afternoon, the first thing my mother told me was that a friend of hers had passed away.

"Who called you and told you the news?" I asked.

"No one called me," she answered.

I was a bit confused. The only person I knew who had recently passed away was Irene's mother, Mrs. LaGravanece. Irene worked for me.

"Irene won't be stopping to see me anymore. Her mother passed away."

"Mom, how do you know?"

"She came to say goodbye," she said.

"Who came to say goodbye?" I asked.

"Irene's mother. She told me she wasn't sorry she had to go, but to let Irene know that she was fine."

When I went to Mrs. LaGravanece's wake, I relayed my mother's message to Irene. Through her tears she expressed her gratitude at my words since she was upset that her mother had been alone when she passed over.

Later that evening, I phoned Avis, the private nurse who attended my mother. I asked how Mom was doing, and Avis informed me that my mother wanted to speak with me.

During our conversation, Mom made a curious request. She asked me to bring three white buttons, a needle, and white thread to the hospital the following day. When I asked why she needed these things, she explained that she had promised the lady she would sew on her three white buttons. I did not question her any further and promised to bring the items she requested. When I arrived at the hospital the next day, Mom immediately asked me for the buttons, needle and thread.

"The lady said she will return soon, so I want to have them here when she comes back," Mom told me.

I asked her, "Who is this lady?"

"The lady said she'll come back to help me."

"When is she coming back?" I asked, still puzzled.

"When it's my time she told me she would return," Mom replied.

Deathbed visions sometimes come from angelic figures sent by a loved one who has passed over earlier, or the presence can be in the form of a religious figure such as Jesus, Moses, or the Blessed Mother. I later realized that Mom's "lady" was the Blessed Mother, and that the three buttons she requested signified the third day of April.

As the final weekend of March neared, Mom asked to speak to each member of the family individually, and announced to each of us that she was going to die. My mother spoke to my sister first. I do not know the details of her conversation, only that she told Connie that she would take over the role of mother to the family and watch over all of us.

One by one we were given our final instructions. When it was my turn, she said, "I really have something to say to you. I love you and I wish things could have been different. It's not that I love the others less, but I'll always love you more. When the time comes, I don't want you to spend too much money."

"Mom, I just want you to remember that when it's my time, I want you to be there in the light to help guide me through."

After our exchange, the rest of the family came back into the room. One of the nurses was summoned because Mom's vital signs were dropping. With growing dread, I knew I was not yet ready to hand her over to God. Desperately trying to win time, I told her that she needed to speak to her sister Rosalie. I dialed my aunt's number and they spoke, then we placed a call to her brother Joe. Her final phone call was to my sister Carol. Carol begged her to hang on a few more days until she flew in from Florida.

For the next few days, Mom continued to speak openly about her passing and to inquire if her dress was finished.

"When it's time for me to go, I have to do this by myself," she reminded me. "I don't wish to have anyone with me."

When Carol finally arrived from Florida, it seemed that my mother had made a full recovery. She even asked Carol to put on her eye shadow and lipstick. When I walked into the room I was stunned—I had not seen my mother look so well in months. With her makeup on, there were no telltale signs of her illness. Even her manner had changed: she was more alert, talkative, and never mentioned dying. Carol turned to me and said, "Doesn't Mommy look beautiful?"

It was not that I did not want my mother to look beautiful and healthy; I had grown accustomed to seeing her in pain. To see her look well and yet know that she was dying made me briefly believe that she was not really sick. But then Carol removed the makeup and it was as if the clock had struck twelve. Just like the Cinderella story, once again Mom looked like her former self, drained and weak.

When someone dies slowly, it is probably easier on the loved ones left behind than a sudden death that leaves the survivors in shock. Our family had months to grow accustomed to Mom's passing and to discuss all the wonderful things that she would witness in her next life. My mother's final wish was to die at home. I was determined to see that her wish was honored. After I obtained her doctor's permission, my mother was released on April 2, 1987.

We arranged to have oxygen delivered, along with all the necessary prescriptions and equipment that was needed to keep her comfortable. I was not on hand to see her leave the hospital in a wheelchair. I simply could not cope with witnessing her weakness and frailty. When the ambulance arrived in front of my mother's home, I was standing outside waiting for her. As a crowd gathered on the sidewalk and the ambulance driver opened the door, I stepped inside. In keeping with her wishes, I asked the nurse to cover her completely with a blanket to shield her from the crowd of people watching.

As we entered the hall to carry her up the stairs, I knew who I would see on the landing. There stood Great-grandma Lily, my final confirmation that Mom's time had come. I could feel the terrible countdown starting. It would only be one more day before my mother passed over.

In a flash we whisked Mom upstairs and tucked into her bed. When she saw her emaciated reflection in the mirror, she wailed, "Oh my God, I didn't think it would be like this."

I did not mention to anyone that I'd spotted Great-grandma Lily in the hall. After being home only about ten minutes, Mom asked to see her father. I went up to the next floor and brought Grandpa down to visit his failing daughter.

Mom asked me to watch over my grandparents and to make certain they had everything they needed. We tried to make small talk with the family, but it was very difficult for everyone. When it was time for me to leave, my mother reminded me that one day I would lie next to her and not to forget all that she had asked.

"And remember that I will love you for all eternity," she said softly.

Although we were relieved that my mother was safely at home, for me the clock was moving too quickly. The next day was April 3. Before leaving the store the next morning, I instructed one of my employees to call the priest so that he could give my mother her last rites. When he arrived in Mom's room and began intoning the ancient ritual, his voice was very loud. When he called my mother's name, she opened her eyes, looked toward him and waved him away. I am sure that he did not realize that she was preoccupied with aligning her inner vision to God's White Light. The priest finished the ritual, said his farewells and left.

Anthony, Connie and Carol were called to the house. As I greeted Connie at the door, I warned her that Mom was fading quickly. She nodded that she understood, then bent and kissed my mother. Connie told Mom how much she loved her and whispered that it was okay for her to go. There was no reply. Mom looked as if she were in a deep sleep. As Connie straightened after her goodbye kiss, her starched collar caught my mother's eyelid. I saw that the murky discoloration had left Mom's eyes. They had returned to the clear blue I had always remembered. This was my confirmation that my mother's transition was complete.

I took my turn with a farewell kiss and whispered all the things I wanted to say. I reminded Mom that when it was my turn she had promised to be there to help me walk into the Light of God. A moment later, I heard the phone ring and answered it. It was my sister Carol calling from Kennedy International Airport. "Mommy just passed away, didn't she?" Carol asked. "I saw her. She came to say goodbye to me at the airport."

I could hear her crying and asked her to come home as quickly as possible. I stepped into the hallway as Anthony was running up the stairs yelling, "Did I make it, did I make it?"

When I answered that he was too late, we melted into each other's arms and wept. We entered the bedroom and everyone started crying all over again. With each new arrival, more tears began to flow. By Monday morning, all of us were exhausted, drained of emotion, and silently relieved that the wake was over and the burial would take place. None of us could tolerate the strain of another hour.

The last memory I have of the day we buried Mom was the stillness of the air and the sun glistening on the bed of pink roses placed on top of her casket.

After my mother passed on, I had one curious dream about

her. She was dressed all in white and was working in a veterinarian's office.

"Mom, what are you doing here?" I asked.

"All good things come in time."

"You haven't answered my question, Mom. What are you doing in a veterinarian's office?"

"All good things come in time," she replied again.

For the next couple of days the dream haunted me. What did it mean? I got my answer one morning when Sandy, our beloved Shetland sheepdog, died. I had to think about the connection between the dog and my dream, but finally understood that my mother's appearance in the vet's office was symbolic of the expression "All God's creatures go to heaven." Sandy had ascended.

One example of how spirits of the departed remind us to remember them happened in the person of a two-year-old.

My family still owns the building in which my grandparents and mother lived. The tenants who live on the top floor have a child named Amanda. During Mother's Day week, 1997, Amanda's parents believed that she was having an imaginary conversation. They heard then two-year-old Amanda say, "Mama, Mama, Mama."

Thinking Amanda was addressing her, Amanda's mother answered, "Yes, Amanda."

Again Amanda said insistently, "No—Mama, Mama, Mama."

The mystery was solved on Mother's Day, when the two-year-old came to my store to visit her father, Billy, one of my employees. On the wall there was a photograph of my mother. Amanda looked up at the photograph, pointed and exclaimed, "Mama!" Then she looked around, smiled at the people in the store, pointed tenderly at the picture and repeated, "Mama, Mama, Mama."

The message the little one was bringing was unraveled: she had visited with my deceased mother and confirmed it by pointing to her photo in the store.

15. THE FIRE

After the long, drawn-out months of my mother's illness, I now had more hours available in the day for myself. I found I did not know what to do with my time. And I discovered that there was little comfort from the pain of my loss. As usual, there were customers to deal with, some of whom didn't know of my mother's passing. It was painful to have to answer their questions and to repeat the same story again and again. I learned that my mother had touched many lives through her kindness, compassion and generosity.

During the next year, for reasons I didn't quite understand, it seemed that the universe shut down my psychic awareness until a day in July 1988. Evidently, I needed to deal with the grief process, including the various stages of anger and acceptance, before my foresight would return.

After Mom's death, Connie moved into a new home and furnished it with things my mother had left behind for her. When I entered her house for the first time, I was apprehensive about seeing my mother's furniture in another setting. I walked into the kitchen and in my mind's eye I suddenly saw flames. I quickly pushed this disturbing image from my mind and said a prayer. The next day I received a phone call at the store. A fire had engulfed a portion of Connie's home. I rushed over and was relieved that she wasn't hurt.

As I entered the house, I wondered why I hadn't warned her the day before. The whole interior of the house was destroyed. The kitchen, where the fire began, was an ashen shell. The dining room was destroyed, except for the laminated prayer cards from my mother's funeral. They were untouched by the flames. Immediately, I remembered what my father had told me on his last visit twenty-three years earlier: "One day all your mother's worldly possessions will burn." As I left the house, I thought it was indeed strange that the television and VCR had been melted by the intense heat, yet the plastic prayer cards had survived.

I came to the conclusion after this tragedy that my psychic awareness had reawakened. Of course, I did not know what visions were yet to come. I thanked God that there had been no messages during that one-year period, because my emotional, physical and mental energies needed balance and rest.

I did receive a call from my friend Frank Castelluccio, saying that his mother, Anna, needed open-heart surgery. He wanted to know from me what the outcome would be. I told him that the surgery would go well and his mother would be fine. Anna Castelluccio came through her surgery like a champ. In this case, I was grateful that my gift of sight was back. I realized that this ability, even though it brought painful truths, helped many people. I sincerely wanted to be of assistance, I just did not know where to start.

My journey began by assisting my friends. As they called me asking for guidance, I received messages from the universe in various ways. They came through my inner voice, visions, spirit guides, and a silent "knowing" that comes without explanation.

One of the calls I received was from a despondent friend who was worried about his finances. In fact, he wanted to die because he was facing bankruptcy. As the reading unfolded, I was advised by the universe that my friend's finances would completely turn around after he filed for bankruptcy. I was told that his new business venture in mid-1990 would manifest endless amounts of money. I advised him to declare bankruptcy; then later, if he chose, he could repay the debts. Today he owns a successful product that appears on national television.

I changed my usual route to work on the morning of March 12. I got off the Verrazano Bridge at the first exit and made a right turn onto 86th Street. At 14th Avenue and 86th Street I stopped for a red light. On the left-hand side of the street was Scarpaci Funeral Home. As I waited for the light to change, I envisioned the funeral home draped in black, and I realized Mr. Scarpaci would be passing soon. His daughter Lena and I are good friends. Lena is a funny, delightful woman who can make the sourest person laugh. Our conversations were usually full of jokes and laughter. Unfortunately, her next call to me was to announce her father's passing.

After Mr. Scarpaci's death, once again my old fear set in and with it my strong recollection of the harsh condemnation of the Catholic priest who said, "Your blood runs cold like a vampire." I had always assumed that this superstitious man had meant that my ability to see death approaching was an unnatural or evil gift.

On the morning of April 11, 1989, as I was driving to work, I heard my mother's voice in my head. "Go visit Grandpa," she said.

"No," I answered.

"Please, go visit Grandpa," she repeated.

"Mom, I really can't deal with this again."

Once again she asked, "Please, go visit Grandpa."

I continued my drive and parked in front of my business. However, my mother's voice came again, this time more insistent. "GO VISIT GRANDPA."

"Okay, Mom," I said out loud.

I went into the store and told my employees that I was going to visit my grandparents. As I entered the downstairs hallway, I dreaded my next steps. I knew that I would see Great-grandma Lily waiting for me. I took a deep breath and started up the stairs. There were no words exchanged between us as I passed her, a gentle apparition with a knowing smile.

My grandmother was sitting at the dining room table and was happy to see me. I rarely visited them after my mother passed, but there were daily telephone calls. I avoided them because of the simple fact that it was too difficult for me to pass Mom's former apartment on the first floor.

"My favorite grandson is here," Grandma said, smiling.

"Hi Grandma, how are you doing?"

"Is there anything wrong?" she asked.

"No, Grandma."

She looked at me strangely, "Are you sure?"

"Grandma, would I tell you a lie?"

"Not my favorite grandson. Would you like coffee? How about toast and eggs?"

"No thank you, Grandma, I have to go back to work, but I wanted to come visit you and Grandpa."

"Grandpa's in the bedroom, he has a cold."

Grandpa looked so thin and drawn lying in bed that I was shaken. I spoke very loudly and called out, "Grandpa."

There was no reply. Once again I heard my mother's voice: "Shave Grandpa."

"I don't want to," I protested.

"Please, shave Grandpa," she pleaded.

"No."

I stayed with my grandpa for a while, then I returned to the dining room. The coffee cups were already on the table and I could smell buttered toast.

"Grandma, I really can't stay very long."

However, I lingered long enough for coffee and toast. As I was driving back to the store, Mom's voice insisted, "Please, go back and shave Grandpa. And cut his nails," she added.

"I'll shave him, but I'm not cutting Grandpa's nails."

I guess that was my mother's way of winning. She knew that if she made two requests, I would comply with one.

"I'll have Connie cut his nails, but I won't do it. If I cut his nails that means I'm getting him ready to pass on."

This may have been my personal superstition, but I truly did not want to be part of my grandfather's passing, and I certainly was not ready to cope with death once again. But as I pulled up to the store, I knew I could no longer ignore my mother's request. I immediately called my grandmother and told her that I would be back later to shave Grandpa. I also called Connie to tell her that I did not think that Grandpa would live until the next day.

"Ed, please do not say that," Connie pleaded. "Is this one of your visions?"

"Make sure that you visit with him after work," I told her.

Next, I dialed Aunt Carol's number and she agreed to go to my grandparents' house.

When I returned to my grandparents' I expected to see Great-grandma Lily in the hall once again, but this time it was empty. I hurried up the stairs and went straight into the bedroom. Grandma was standing near the bed trying to give Grandpa a sip of water. I took out the cordless shaver and shaved him.

"Grandpa looks so much better clean-shaven," Grandma told me.

I washed his face. I noticed that his breathing seemed to be more labored.

Aunt Carol arrived and Connie soon after. I reminded Connie to cut his nails, but did not tell her about hearing my mother's voice, or about seeing Great-grandma Lily in the hall. Aunt Carol decided she would call the doctor. He arrived shortly, a young man who was not familiar with our family.

"He should really be in the hospital," he said after a brief examination. "He has pneumonia. I'm going to give him an injection, then I'll try to reach his doctor and have him admitted into the hospital."

"Doctor, before you give my grandfather anything, don't you realize he is dying and the injection or a hospital is not going to do anything for him?" I asked.

"This man has pneumonia," the doctor replied.

"My grandfather has the death rattle," I told him.

He looked at me, and I could see he was angry. He replied, "I'm the doctor here."

"I mean no disrespect, but look at my grandfather's feet."

He turned back the blanket and examined my grandfather's feet, then looked at me and said, "Sir, I'm terribly sorry, you are correct. This man is dying."

"My grandfather won't last until tomorrow morning," I informed him.

The doctor asked me if I had ever studied medicine, and how I was able to make an accurate diagnosis. Too caught up in the situation to make up an excuse, I surprised myself and told him flat out that I received information from the universe. I'm sure my answer surprised him, too.

I stayed with Grandpa for two more hours and said my good-byes. I silently spoke to my mother, telling her how much she was missed and that I knew Grandpa would be with her before morning. And once again, I needed to ask her not to forget when my turn came to be there for me.

The next morning, the phone rang at seven-thirty. I was asked to hurry to my grandparents' house because grandpa did not look well and his breathing was very shallow. When I arrived, my grandfather had already passed away. Later, as I thought of my grandfather with fondness and love, I realized he had had more time on earth than many people. He was one hundred years old when he passed into God's White Light.

PART TWO

REACHING OUT

16. A NEW PATH

*M*y friend Aggie had visited George, a psychic channeler and prominent medium. When she returned from her session with him, she was excited and told a mutual friend about her experience. Intrigued, we scheduled an appointment. Like most people about to visit a psychic, I was excited and hoped I would not be disappointed. I didn't know that this event would change the path of my life.

When I arrived, there were about twenty people sitting on folding chairs in a long, narrow room. I sat down next to Aggie. As George began his readings, he gave people information about their loved ones and explained how they passed over. He was three chairs away from where I was sitting when a spirit child came to me and spoke.

"My name is Eric," the child said. "I died in a car crash."

Meanwhile, George was speaking to Eric's parents about their teenage son, telling them that he was athletic. "He was here a moment ago, where did he go?" George asked.

Of course, the boy had slipped away to speak to me.

"Oh, here he is." George said. "His name begins with an E."

"His name is Eric," I whispered to Aggie. "He died in an automobile accident."

"How do you know?" Aggie asked.

"Because he just told me."

A split second after I said those words George said, "His name is Eric. He died in a car accident."

His parents, who were present in the room, began to cry. When it was my turn for George to speak to me, I trusted him because Eric's appearance had proved his reliability. I still did not believe wholly in my own psychic powers. He did not know that Aggie and I were together.

George told me my mother's name was Mary and that she said

hello to me. My dad came through George next and apologized for teasing me when I was a child. As George spoke my father's words, I could feel myself reacting with the same old anger. I realized I still had not forgiven him and that I had to work on my hostile feelings. It wasn't too much later that I reached a point in my life where I did forgive my father, allowing love and respect to come to the front.

That day in the room with George, something powerful stirred in me. It was so reassuring to know that there was another person who also spoke to spirits. And what's more, George didn't fear delivering his profound messages. As I watched each face in the room glow from his reassuring words, I realized how much comfort he gave to the bereaved group. Through him they were linked to their loved ones. My own doorway to a new path was now fully opened.

On my new path, a remarkable psychic, Shoshana, came into my life. Her consultations, coaching and teaching opened a much broader spiritual vista for me to contemplate. With her inspiration, I learned to trust the messages that came to me from the other world, in which God's Light is a bright beacon. As my year working with Shoshana progressed, I could sense a weight being lifted from my heart. I came to know that we are all mirror reflections of one another. It is important to understand this concept because, when another person is in pain, he may project his pain onto you.

My new path was to hold many miraculous adventures. I began to travel with a renewed sense of commitment to learning and experiencing as much as I could in order that I might be blessed in my experiences and increase my understanding of all things paranormal. I was certain I had much to learn before I could go out and help others, and I knew that what I needed most to learn about was me.

The first of my discovery trips was to Canada to see the Crystal Skull of Atlantis, owned by a woman named Anna Mitchell Hedges. Since 1927, she has been the custodian of this incredibly beautiful and powerful artifact. The story was that she had been on an expedition with her father in the jungle of Belize, believed to be part of the continent of Atlantis. There she came upon a ruined temple whose altar had been buried by fallen stone and got her first glimpse of a shiny object that turned out to be the skull. She was all of sixteen years old. On her seventeenth birthday in 1924, the skull was retrieved. According to legend, it had been lost for a thousand years.

The Hedges Skull was carved from a fifty-pound block of clear crystal. The skull maintains an even temperature of seventy degrees whether it is placed in a freezing compartment or subjected to high heat. In the skull, it is said one can see ancient civilizations, objects moving through the air, people getting on and off spaceships, and prehistoric animals unknown to man. It has been suggested that people who are especially drawn to the Hedges Skull have known it before.

On seeing the skull myself, I witnessed something that would alter my life for years to come. What I glimpsed was the initial vision that would lead me to write this book. Still, I was often resistant to what I felt called to do. Two perfect examples of this came in the guise of two trips. The first would take me to Sedona, Arizona, said to be a psychic vortex that possesses magical, supernatural energies.

In Sedona, I met a Native American shaman who invited me to take part in the rituals of a sweat lodge. Sweats take place in a small circular structure made of canvas. A central pit is dug in the earth. Rocks are heated in an outside fire and then brought in and thrown into the pit. Water is then thrown on and the steam, scented with sage and various herbs, fills the lodge. Of the several people involved in the sweat, each are assigned specific responsibilities. Mine was to tend the fire. I was to carry hot rocks from the outside fire to the inner pit with a pitchfork. With the intense heat and chanting, it is not uncommon to enter an altered state of consciousness inside the sweat lodge. One can experience visions and confront the very nature of one's fears. As the shaman drummed and chanted, I began to have a past life recall of a lifetime spent in Egypt. I suddenly felt as if huge water bugs were crawling all over my skin. I did not realize at the time that such insects were called scarabs and considered sacred. The scarab is a large, dark beetle worshipped in ancient Egypt. I could also see myself being placed in a stone sarcophagus. My sense of being buried alive felt all too real as the huge stone slab slid over the top of the sarcophagus, and I began to panic. I quickly picked myself up and ran out of the lodge, not realizing that it was forbidden to leave during the ceremony. Needless to say, the shaman was upset with me. But he was polite enough to excuse my behavior. He told me that as the fire bearer, I was only allowed to leave once. When I came back in I would not be allowed to leave again. I took a few deep breaths of the cool air outside the lodge before making my way back in. When I returned, it seemed the shaman began to drum and chant much harder. I stayed in for the duration. Even though I tried to run from the feeling, it turned out to be one of the most profound experiences of my life.

My next trip was to Egypt. After my experience in the sweat lodge and the memory of the sarcophagus and the crawling scarabs, it seemed only a matter of time before I was to find myself stepping into the land of the pharaohs. It was a trip I was determined not to take. But my inner guidance made it clear that I must. I could not understand why I fought so hard not to go, as it turned out to be one of the most extraordinarily spiritual trips I could ever imagine. I was somehow brought home to myself. Indeed, I felt that I had come home when I arrived in Egypt. The pyramids did not look foreign. Ramses II's temple did not feel unfamiliar, either. It was as though I had walked through those pillars many times before. Even the hieroglyphics made some kind of sense to me, though obviously I could not interpret them literally. When I was able to finally enter the King's Chamber of the Great Pyramid itself, my soul was flooded by memories of the Gods.

In fact, I had not read much about ancient Egypt and didn't know much about the culture or the history. Yet, when I looked around me, all that went through my head was, "Look what they've done to my Egypt." I could only think of all the great changes that had taken place since I once walked in a previous life on Egyptian soil. I remembered what Signora Maria had told me about a past life in Egypt and recalled what I had felt those hours in the sweat lodge. Now I was feeling the remnants of that life and observing the scarabs in their natural habitat.

On our itinerary was a trip across the Red Sea and a climb up Mount Sinai. Though it seemed like a rather daunting hike, I started the climb along with the rest of my group. Most of them were to make it to the top within five hours, just before sunrise. I made it to the top just as the sun started to rise. I was thankful it had taken me the little extra time, for when I got to the top I felt as though I were arriving at the very house of God himself. The sky trumpeted with an unforgettably glorious hue. On the top of Mount Sinai there is a small place of worship. I was a little surprised when everyone did not drop to their knees to give thanks to God, because I was intent on praying on that very spot. The universal energy was everywhere evident on the top of that mountain. I considered the climb a small offering for all that the Creator had done for us.

17. SWEET SPIRIT

On the thirty-second anniversary of my father's death, June 16, 1992, I began public readings. One of my first readings was for a man named John. The woman from the spirit world who came forward to communicate with John was a sweet, gentle soul. I was confused at first because I saw her as a photograph negative, then I realized she was African-American.

I informed John that she had taken care of him when he was a child during a period while he was ill. John became upset and said, "I don't believe you."

I thanked the spirit for coming, but she insisted that I give John a final message.

She said, "Tell him my only son was found hanged."

John's eyes flew open; shock flooded his face. "I will never doubt again," John said. "What she said is absolutely true. This woman was my nanny and I loved her dearly."

Connections with souls who have gone to the other side often occur in surprising circumstances. One evening I was sitting in a restaurant with a friend, Steve, when a young man came to our table.

"I'm sorry to disturb you, but I'm here in New York on business and I'm not familiar with this area. Can you tell me how to get to Lincoln Center?"

After giving him the directions, he put out his hand. "My name is Tom," he said.

As I shook his hand, my thumb rested on top of a diamond that was set in his ring. Suddenly I experienced a strange sensation, and the right side of my mouth dropped as if an invisible hand had pulled it downward. I wiped my lower lip as I spoke. Afflicted with this odd facial deformity, I began telling the young man about his grandfather, who was the original owner of the ring.

What you're doing with your lip is amazing," Tom said. "My grandfather used to look like that."

I apologized for my expression. I couldn't explain it.

"If you do not mind, would you continue?" Tom asked.

"For whatever wrong your grandfather did to your family, he is truly sorry," I told him. "When he became crippled, he blamed your father, and he wanted to make your whole family suffer. He made your life miserable."

Tom nodded in acknowledgment, then said that he loved his grandfather and he was grateful that he was apologizing. "Does he know how much I love him?" Tom asked.

"Tom, he says he loves you, too."

Renee, the hostess in the restaurant, had overheard our conversation. As we were leaving she stopped me and said rather brazenly, "I hear you're a psychic." I confirmed this, wondering where this was going.

"Can you tell me something?" she asked.

"Yes," I answered. "Your grandfather Solomon wishes to say hello."

"That is my grandfather's name!" she screamed.

Then I continued on a serious note. "I don't wish to frighten you, but one day there will be a difficulty with one of your breasts. You mustn't be concerned. It will not be cancerous," I promised her.

Approximately two years later, a lump was to develop in the woman's breast. Walking back home after the mammogram, she recalled what I had said to her two years earlier. She was grateful for the message she had received. It enabled her to remain calm while she waited for the results of her test. She was told it was a harmless fibroid tumor.

18. CALLING CARL

*T*hose of us who are sensitive to spirits of the dead often attract those who have a difficult time making the transition from life as we know it to the unknown. Often, people who have died but are distraught because they think they have left unfinished business on Earth, attempt to delay or resist their passage to the beyond. The story that follows relates how one such reluctant spirit desperately sought to reverse the circumstances of his death.

I learned about the death of Carl from his widow in Seattle several years after the event. She related the story of an astonishing telephone call from a friend, three thousand miles away, barely twelve hours after her husband's demise.

Margaret, still stunned and bewildered by the violent death of her husband the previous morning, had fallen into an exhausted sleep after a confusing, depressing day of trying to find answers to questions about why her husband had died. They were questions that baffled and disturbed her and plunged her deeper into grief and misery. When the telephone on her nightstand rang at two o'clock in the morning, she groped for the receiver, groggy and disoriented. Still drugged with sleep, unaware of the early morning hour, she thought she was receiving another condolence call. During the day there had been dozens of expressions of shock and sympathy from friends and relatives.

When she sat up in bed to place the receiver against her ear, she noticed the early hour on her bedside clock. Margaret was surprised and mystified when her caller turned out to be a family friend, Natalie. What was she doing on the phone from New York at such an ungodly hour? She barely acknowledged Natalie's greeting when her friend, with unaccustomed rude urgency, said, "Margaret, I have to talk with Carl. I know it's early, but I've got to talk with him! Please put him on the phone."

Natalie, a woman who had stayed with Margaret and Carl for

a prolonged period two years previously, had proven to be a provocative house guest with strong spiritual leanings. Her remarkable powers of clairvoyance sometimes made a startling appearance over breakfast coffee. One morning, Natalie had suddenly put her cup down firmly on the breakfast table and, with a strange light in her eyes, turned to Margaret and said, "Irene is dead."

"What do you mean? You're crazy! How would you know such a thing? I just talked to her yesterday!"

Natalie was referring to a dear friend of Margaret's who had originally introduced Natalie to Margaret. She had moved to Los Angeles from Seattle to assist her daughter in a medical subscription business. Margaret and Irene had been close friends since they studied together years before at the University of Washington.

Unmoved by Margaret's dismayed rejection of her announcement, Natalie had said softly, "I'm sorry you took the news badly, but it's true. Irene's dead. I can't tell you how I know, but she's gone."

Still unbelieving, but worried and concerned, Margaret had called Irene's number in Los Angeles. When the phone was answered, she immediately recognized Sally, Irene's daughter.

"Sally, is your mother all right? It's Margaret."

"Oh, Margaret," Sally cried, "I'm so glad it's you. Mom died this morning. A stroke. I don't know what to do! Will you come?"

Now, two years later, with Natalie's former prediction of Irene's death in her mind as a warning, Margaret said to her friend on the Atlantic coast, "Why such a hurry to speak to Carl? Why are you so disturbed?"

There was a long moment of hesitation on the line before Natalie's voice came back. "Margaret, I was awakened just a few minutes ago. At first, I thought it was a dream, then I realized it wasn't. It was Carl. He was standing at the foot of my bed. His head was thickly bandaged and blood had soaked through the gauze and was running down his face.

"At first," she continued, "I thought it couldn't be Carl

because he was wearing a shadow plaid suit with a paisley tie. He never dressed like that. He always wore conservative suits, pin-striped blue or gray. Then, I realized it was him. Oh, Margaret, his eyes were terrible to look at, full of pain and regret when he asked for help. He was desperate and kept saying, 'Help me, Natalie. Help me get back. I've done something awful and I have to get back. I've made a terrible mistake.'

"He disappeared and then came back again in a few minutes," said Natalie. "He kept pleading for me to help him. He was so pitiful and desperate, I thought my heart would break. I couldn't make up my mind whether I was dreaming, or if his visit was real. I knew I had to call and find out what was tormenting him. Is he there?"

Margaret sighed deeply from the hard knot of sadness and hurt that burned her chest and threatened to engulf her with grief. She took a deep, ragged breath, then said shakily to Natalie, "Oh my dear, he's not here anymore. He went to his office early yester-day morning, sat at his desk, put a gun to his head and pulled the trigger. He's dead, Natalie. And yesterday morning he dressed in a new shadow plaid suit he had bought, and put on a silly paisley tie. He looked so different, as if he wasn't himself at all. Of course, he wasn't. You had no way of knowing what happened. It hasn't been on the news or anything like that."

It was several days after Natalie's call that Margaret thought about her husband's visitation to their friend in New York. Not for a moment did she doubt his appearance in Natalie's bedroom, begging her for help to return from across the gulf of the dead. Margaret concluded that Carl's desperate appearance after he'd killed himself was his renunciation of his act and prayer for for-giveness. He had gone to the one person he knew of who would not have dismissed his nocturnal vision as an aberration or a bad dream that should be ignored.

As she sat down alone in her bedroom after Carl's funeral, after all the busyness and ceremony and etiquette of death obser-vance had been dutifully completed, and after she had overcome her own exhaustion in a deep, healing sleep, Margaret made a tentative peace with her husband's suicide. She accepted that he had killed himself because of cruel changes in the executive lineup at the corporation to which he had devoted twenty-five years of his life. He was being mercilessly pushed out, discarded, and he was terrified of the future.

She had accepted this explanation with irony, feeling deep regret for him and a certain bitterness over his wasting his life because he felt desperately inadequate compared to men who were far less than him. She understood how he could think of no solution but to arrange for his own absence. More significant and deeply profound to her was his strange appearance in the New York apartment of their friend after he died. She had always hoped—not really believed—that life continued after death, but now her husband had left her with a gift he had not intended—the certainty that life is ongoing. She was convinced that death is but a stage in human development. It was a sweet knowledge for Margaret, and it gave her husband's death a greater meaning than the rude ending in his office.

19. STRANGER AT THE AIRPORT

*A*t a dinner party at my home in Staten Island one evening, one of the dinner guests, a remarkable woman, told a story about a friend of hers that fascinated everybody at the table. Here is what she told us about Martha.

Shortly after a thorough medical checkup following her complaint of a sore spot high on her shoulder blade, Martha's doctor asked her to come into his office. As soon as she was seated in a chair in front of his desk, Dr. Claude Burger said to his patient, "Martha, I've never been good at breaking bad news, but the fact is I have some disturbing information to give you."

A little shaken, Martha, a slender fifty-one-year-old mother of three grown children, with a husband she loved and a flower shop she was devoted to, sat a little straighter in her chair. She looked directly into her physician's eyes. "All right, doctor, what's the matter with me?"

Dr. Burger clasped his hands together on his desk and said, "It's the sore spot on your right shoulder. I could show you on the x-rays we took, if you like, but, well, it's cancerous. And it's the fast-growing kind. Already it's metastasized and that means we can't stop it."

He paused, and Martha leaned forward in her chair. "You're sure about this? I mean, there's no question in your mind that it's fatal?"

"No, Martha, there's no question. I've had five radiologists examine the x-rays and they all agree. Of course, you can, probably should, get another opinion . . ."

"I don't think that'll be necessary," Martha replied. "I trust you. You've always been honest and straightforward with us. How long do I have?"

"It's hard to tell, Martha. I'd say three, maybe four months."

"Oh dear, that soon?"

"Yes."

Martha left her physician's office and drove directly home instead of opening her flower shop in southwest Boston. She phoned her assistant, Laura, at her apartment, and explained she had been delayed. Would Laura open the shop and take care of the pending orders? Martha said the delay might be prolonged. She thanked Laura and sat down in the kitchen and sipped cold breakfast coffee. She was slightly amazed at her calm. Her death had been predicted by a steady, reliable physician whose eyes had mirrored his distress and sympathy. Four months, probably three, and she would be gone. How could that be? A devout Catholic who rarely missed Mass, who could quote many passages from the Bible when she chose, Martha was surprised at the emptiness in her head. Certainly, she thought, some profound expression of loss should rise from her mind to console her, but all she could think of was that she had forgotten to take out the kitchen garbage from under the sink.

It was much later that day when George, her husband, came home from his work as a lumber broker and she broke the news to him. After her announcement, when George recovered from the initial shock and finality of the doctor's verdict, the two of them sat subdued and blank-faced in their living room. Martha broke the silence between them when she said she had decided not to tell their children about her shortened life expectancy. "They'll discover it for themselves soon enough," she explained, then added, "I'd like for us to go away for awhile, George. We've been promising ourselves a vacation, but we keep putting it off. Now's the perfect time, dear." And so, George and Martha left for three weeks, praised by their children for being sensible and good to themselves.

It was when they returned from their vacation and walked from their flight into Boston International Airport that a strange event happened. Martha whispered to George that she wanted to freshen up in the ladies' restroom, and left him to wait in the passenger seating area. A few minutes later, just as Martha began her return trip to George from across the wide passenger walkway, a small, rather timid man with a pale face and a kind, friendly expression stepped up to George and said, "Pardon me, sir, but I have a message for your wife. Do you mind if I give it to her personally? I see her coming across the way." George briefly inspected the inoffensive little man who stood in front of him. He was slender, dressed in a dark suit and a white shirt with a small, neat tie. His face was pleasant and topped with ginger hair. He certainly did not appear to offer any kind of threat. Oddly, George would remember later that he felt no sense of curiosity about the message for his wife or the messenger.

The stranger intercepted Martha as she approached her husband, and he said to her courteously, "Martha, I have an important message for you. You must believe it. You are going to be perfectly all right. There is nothing for you to worry about. You are fine and nothing is going to happen to you." Before Martha could comment or ask the stranger who he was, he smiled at her, gave her a farewell salute with his right hand, and briskly walked away, soon swallowed in a crowd of passengers.

Of course, Martha told George about the little man's urgent declaration, and during their taxi ride from the airport to their home they discussed and pondered the meaning of the stranger's visit. Secretly, in her heart, Martha had been deeply moved by the messenger's sincerity, the absolute conviction in his voice that she was going to be perfectly all right. She wondered, then decided with rising hope and with a strange certainty that the messenger's firm affirmation was a direct, indisputable reference to her state of health.

When the couple arrived home and collected their phone messages, Martha and George were overwhelmed with excitement by the voice of Dr. Claude Burger: "Martha, call me at home as soon as you get back. I've got good news for you. My number is . . . ."

The news from Martha's physician was like a burst of sunlight in a room darkened with hopelessness. Instead of a metastasized cancer on her right shoulder, which had been confirmed by five radiologists, the cancer was a rare variety that on film and under a microscope bore a striking resemblance to the more deadly and terminal disease diagnosed by the radiologists. Martha's physician, struggling to accept the death verdict he had pronounced on his patient, had sent a set of the x-rays to an oncologist in San Francisco. While George and Martha were on their vacation, the oncologist had called Dr. Burger. "I'm delighted to tell you boys that your diagnosis is in error. I hope you haven't notified the patient of your findings." In the telephone conversation with Martha to tell her his good news, Dr. Burger informed her that a simple operation of a few minutes to excise the cancer from her back was all that stood between her and excellent health. He would schedule it immediately.

Released from her death sentence, Martha and her husband looked at one another in awe as they remembered the small, slender messenger at the Boston airport who had promised Martha that she was all right. How did he know? Who was he? Where had he come from?

"How did he know my name?" Martha asked.

It was finally her secret conclusion that she had been visited by an angel. He had been sent from God to relieve her burden, to give her the good news. It was not until many years later that Martha confided the strange and miraculous story to her grown daughter.

I love stories such as the one I've just related. And there are many of them that seem to have a principal message all of us should heed: God sends constant reminders, in the form of angels and little miracles, that life doesn't end with death.

I'll never forget the young woman in her late teens who had become totally blind before her final days on earth. She was a devout Christian and loved statues of figures from the scriptures. What amazed visitors who came to see her and brought her miniature replicas of saints like Peter, Paul, Luke and John was her uncanny identification of the statues. Though she never once touched or fondled them, she focused her blind eyes on their tiny figures and confidently named them. Even when some visitors, suspecting a trick, silently moved the statues, she was unperturbed and unfailingly reoriented her gaze, gave them their names and said a prayer. She soon passed on into the White Light of God.

20. TRUST

*I*t was late in March when Louis arrived for his appointment. I looked into his eyes and could see his pain. It was as though his three-year-old inner child had come out of hiding and now stood before me. Louis was feeling a heightened sense of despair and loneliness. He thought he had come alone to the appointment, but the truth of the matter was that a spirit named Martin was also present. Martin's essence was wonderfully prevalent, full of loving energy toward Louis. Martin's first words to me were, "Please help Louis."

It is not important from which disease one passes over, rather it is the judgment of others that surrounds and lends a disease a particular stigma. What is important is what we do with the time we spend on Earth.

"Why do you want to kill yourself?" I asked Louis.

"There is nothing here for me but pain," he answered.

I told Louis that I knew he had been an abused child. He acknowledged that this was true. I thought then about how many things in life seem so unjust. How a trusting and loving child can be unaware that an adult might be misleading him, deviously preparing to cross that child's boundaries. How the pain of a three-year-old can be carried for years, unaware that at the time of the situation they could not have been in control. Still, they suffer as though they had allowed the abuse to happen. In Louis's case, he had been abused as a child by both his parents. One abused him sexually and the other failed to protect him. Furthermore, daily beatings and name-calling by his mother only added to his shaming. I told Louis it was time for him to take off the bandages that had been mummifying his heart and to begin to love himself. The mind is like a computer, and when something is stored, particularly those significant events that occur in our lives, they can be recalled at any given moment. For Louis, the significant event that was beginning to be re-addressed was the crossing over of his father. There had been no healing words between them, no "I'm sorry" to alleviate the pain of the past. When we lose a loved one, within the grief there can be an inner sense of peace due to the fact that the person can no longer hurt us. It is at such a time that the mind often releases all that has been stored.

During Louis's session, many important messages arose. One must deliver what is at hand. It is totally up to the client to take the messages and accept or dismiss them. One such message was a warning for him to change his field of work. Louis confessed he was trying desperately to get out of his line of work as he was unhappy with his profession.

"Louis, you need to make that change tonight—not in a week or a month. Otherwise, you'll be hurting yourself further," I counseled him.

Moments later I received a revelatory flash of Louis amidst bars and guns. A week later Louis was arrested.

I was to get another portentous vision two months afterward when at eight-thirty in the morning my phone rang. I picked it up and could hear Louis's excited voice on the other end of the line.

"Ed, I'm going for a blood test today. Can you please tell me what to expect?"

"Everything will be clear," was my reply. Then I added, "Louis, if I asked you to wait until next week, would you wait?"

"No, I need to go today,"

Around mid-afternoon Louis called me and I could hear him crying. He managed to get out that the test had come out positive and that he had HIV. He wanted to meet with me later that day. When we were together again, I could hear the Blessed Mother telling me to share with Louis a message from Martin. When I was told the message, I asked the Blessed Mother if I was hearing her correctly.

"Trust and deliver the message," was her reply.

"Louis, the Blessed Mother tells me that Martin is with the angels and he says to tell you to 'Send in the Clowns.' " On hearing this, Louis broke down in tears.

"How did you ever get that?" he asked me incredulously.

"Louis, sometimes I am given messages that only the person I am working with will understand," I tried to explain.

Next the Blessed Mother told me to tell Louis that he was HIV negative and that he needed to go back and retake the test. Again, I asked the Blessed Mother if what I was hearing was correct. Once again, she counseled me to trust. Inside, I feared contradicting the doctors, but I chose to trust the Blessed Mother and relay the message. I felt as though I were rescuing Louis from a firing squad. But was it only to place him back again in one week's time? Louis told me he trusted me. Why didn't I have trust in what I heard? I prayed for the next week that it was not my imagination that had told me such a thing. Who was I to give a person such hope?

On the day he was to be retested, I heard our Lady tell me again to have trust. She then said, very clearly, "You will be called at four-forty-five and Louis will tell you he is negative, and then will you believe?"

At four-forty-five the telephone rang. It was Louis. He could barely get the words out of his mouth. All he could say was "Ed, Ed, Ed . . ."

I started to say, "Louis, I'm sorry . . ."

"No, Ed, I'm negative! The funny thing was, I believed you from the moment you told me. You, of all people . . . should trust yourself," Louis insisted wisely.

21. THE MIRACULOUS BEADS

*M*y wife, Prudence, was going to have surgery. The night before, I pinned a string of blue rosary beads to her bedside. The next morning, before she was to be taken to the operating room, I walked into her room and had a vision of my wife's father standing at her bedside stroking her head and smiling. Prudence looked up at me wearily.

"Am I going to die?" she asked.

I smiled at her and assured her she was not going to die.

"You're going to be fine," I told her.

Inside, however, I wondered if the appearance of my father-in-law was not possibly the vision of an angel come to take my wife to God.

As the staff was getting ready to wheel the bed out, I suddenly thought to take the rosary beads off the bed, but when I went to do so, one of the attendants stopped me.

"She'll be back in the same bed. Leave it."

A few hours after the surgery I was allowed to visit my wife in the intensive care unit for a few moments. I noticed immediately that the blue rosary was not there, but had been replaced with a pink one. I asked Prudence what had happened to the blue one.

"I don't know. A lady came and gave me a pink one," said my wife, groggily.

No one had been allowed to visit Prudence before or after her surgery—at least no one from this Earth plane. Evidently, my father-in-law was not the only person watching over Prudence from the other side.

22. THE PRIEST

As I grew more confident of my abilities, I became capable of manifesting or bringing goodness to myself, but I was still unable to let go of one particular fear. Even though I worked with Shoshana and many other wonderful teachers, I was still afraid of the intuitive knowledge that I'd possessed since I was a baby. I knew that I was able to see into the past, present and future and to foresee illness, death and even the beginning of a new life. In the business world I manifested what I needed to provide for my family. However, in the spiritual realm, I was still influenced by the condemning words of the Catholic priest who had cursed me years ago with his assertion that my blood ran cold. It took another priest to free me and teach me that the work I did helped others calm their fears of the unknown. From that priest, I also accepted the assurance that I was destined to help ease the shattering loss and pain that came to people when someone special they loved died.

I was with a friend, Ralph, having a drink one night when a stranger approached me.

"I was told you are a psychic," he said. "And I hope you don't mind the interruption, but I need your help."

"May I feel your vibrations?" I asked. I placed my forefinger and index finger in the center of his palm. "I can only tell you what I hear," I told him. "You can do God's work anywhere."

"What do you mean?" he asked, his face expressionless.

"Excuse me, Father," I said. "In your office, directly in front of your desk, is a large wooden cross. You just left your position with the Church. You were a hierarch in the Roman Catholic Church."

He looked at me and smiled. "You are absolutely correct," he said.

I asked if he would mind if I turned the tables and asked him a question. I told him the story of the priest who had compared me to a vampire.

"Your blood does not run cold," he assured me, smiling. "You're a very gifted man. Don't ever stop sharing your wonderful gift. It comes from God for you to give to the world."

Strangely, it was a priest who embedded the nails of fear in my heart and another who pulled them out and helped soothe the pain. The summer of 1993 was when I finally lost the fear of my special foresight and allowed myself to continue my exploration into the world of the paranormal.

23. PAST LIVES

*I*t wasn't long after my meeting with the second priest that I decided to educate myself about past life regression. I made an appointment to be hypnotized by Dr. George Bien. When I arrived at his office, I was a little apprehensive, wondering if I could be hypnotized at all. The first time we shook hands I could feel that he was warm and honest. He escorted me into his hypnotherapy room, which was equipped with recording gear. He explained that the recording instruments would chronicle the session. I was seated in a comfortable chair when the session began. Dr. Bien spoke very softly. As he talked, his voice resonated deeply in my being. He was a kind and perceptive man.

"Now, I want you to imagine that you are standing inside the door to your home and that you are opening the door," he said. "Imagine that the door opens into a long tunnel and there is a light at the end. I am going to count backwards from twenty to one. I want you to imagine that with each number I speak, you are moving down through the tunnel toward the light. I want you to imagine that you are moving toward the light and back through time to a lifetime you lived previous to this one. And, when I reach the number one, you will step from the tunnel into the light, into that previous lifetime."

As he spoke, I felt myself totally relax. I could hear myself answering his questions, yet I felt disconnected from the outside world. When the session was over, Dr. Bien said that it was a profound experience for him. He told me that at times I did not speak, but the expressions on my face, my laughter and tears were wonderful to watch. He handed me my tape and I thanked him. As I got back into my car, I felt as if the session had only lasted ten minutes. When I looked at the clock on the dashboard, I was astonished to see that an hour and a half had passed.

I took the cassette and placed it into the tape deck. I listened to myself in disbelief. I was describing a past life in a monastery, disclosing details as to what I was wearing. In my hypnotic state I recognized another person from that lifetime as someone who, like me, now lived in the present. I saw that person among a group of people who were working in a field of vegetables. Actually, I did not recognize his face, because it was different from the face he wears in his current life. But I recognized him by his spiritual essence. Toward the end of the tape, Dr. Bien had asked me to go back to the beginning of time. He questioned where I was and what I was looking at. I told him that I could see Earth as if from a great distance, from a location that I thought was the universal realm.

After listening to the taped session, I was still skeptical and doubted if I could be hypnotized (I am a hard-headed kid from Brooklyn, after all). I decided to go to another hypnotist, Bob, and it was from him that I learned that I was a suitable subject for hypnotherapy. As a result of this interview, I was convinced that my regression experiment truly represented another life I had led. Later, I couldn't help but recall Barbra Streisand singing, "On a clear day, rise and look around you, and you'll see who you are . . ."

I have come to understand that we are far more than we think we are. We are spiritual kings and queens, masters of the universe, children of God. Death simply brings us to another version of who we are. If we can truly understand this, imagine what we could do with our lives. Unshackled from the bonds of mortality, we could act and behave as if our souls were truly unlimited, giving us the power that Edna St. Vincent Millay described so superbly in her poem "Renaissance": "The soul can split the sky in two, and let the face of God shine through."

24. ORDAINED

$\mathcal{D}$espite my deepening conviction that I had a gift of seeing that should be shared with others searching for answers about dying, it took me more than a year to decide whether I was worthy of becoming an ordained minister. Part of my dilemma was that I did not want to change my Roman Catholic beliefs, so I decided to become affiliated with an interfaith ministry. The deciding factor was that, as a part of my counseling and healing work, sometimes my clients asked me to perform marriage ceremonies. As an ordained minister, I'd be able to perform that rite and take part in this important celebration in a special way.

Weddings bring me great joy because there is so much love exchanged during a wedding ceremony. Of course, along with the joy in my new designation, there was also sadness. There were those times when I was called on to visit someone who was ill or when a family member requested that I help a loved one pass over.

After I had spent some time going around and around about whether or not to become a minister, a boy became the catalyst for my decision.

I received a phone call informing me that Damion, the son of a friend, had been gravely injured in an automobile accident which had instantly taken his father's life. Rafaela, my friend and Damion's mother, requested that I come to the hospital and perform a healing on Damion. I asked my friends Aggie and Bob to accompany me. As we drove to the hospital in New Jersey, we prayed for Damion.

When we arrived, we were escorted into the intensive care unit. Damion lay in a bed at the far left side of the room. At first it appeared to us that Damion did not have a mark on his body from the accident. I had not seen the left side of his head yet, but I understood it had been crushed in the accident.

There was one particular monitor in the unit that measured

Damion's brain waves. We quickly discovered that the machine was registering activity far above normal. If it remained in the high ranges, Damion would be considered brain dead.

As the three of us began our healing ritual, the monitor dropped to a safe level. The healing work we were doing consisted of transmitting energy from a higher source of power to Damion. There is a wide range of healing techniques to help the injured, including prayer. All of them invoke the help of God. We knew that we were merely conduits drawing down the higher source of power that we directed to Damion. A nurse, who stood behind us observing our actions, answered the question of a young doctor who observed, "Do you see the level of the monitor? What are they doing?"

"Quiet," she said. "They're praying."

When we completed our healing and prayers, we joined Damion's mother, Rafaela, in the family waiting room. She was distraught, not only over the death of her husband, but over the balance between life and death in which her son hovered.

"Ed, what do you think?" Rafaela asked.

"Rafaela, this is Damion's choice," I said. "He can choose to stay here on the Earth plane or to walk into God's White Light."

"With Fred gone, I cannot lose my son, too," she told me, and began sobbing.

We stayed with Rafaela for a while, then returned to the intensive care unit to pray again before leaving for New York. During our second visit, the brain activity monitor indicated a dangerous level in Damion's condition. This time, as we prayed and performed a healing ritual, there was no encouraging movement of the needle.

The next afternoon, I received a call from Rafaela begging me to come back and pray for Damion. She acknowledged to me that the doctors had warned her there was no hope for her son. But Aggie, Bob and I drove to the hospital once again and walked into Damion's room. Even though his body was lying in the bed, I could see his etheric body standing near the bed holding onto a saintly female figure. I knew that Damion was trying to make the decision of whether to go with the Heavenly Mother or stay on.

I spoke to the etheric Damion and said, "It is your choice. Your mom and sisters will be fine."

Neither Bob, Aggie nor I did a healing. We simply prayed for Damion to make his own choice. When I left the room once again, his mother asked me, "Ed, what do you think?"

"Rafaela, I can only tell you what I saw. Damion was with the Blessed Mother. He has to make his own choice. It's tough because he loves you very dearly. Rafaela, sometimes we can hold our loved ones earthbound because of the great love we feel for them."

"I know," she said.

"If you understand that, then you must tell Damion that it's all right to go, so he can feel less held back by your love."

I was not called by Damion's family the next evening. Instead, a Roman Catholic healing priest was asked to visit him. When he left Damion's room to talk with the family, he asked them to stop praying and promised that he would take over their prayers. He said the family's prayers were preventing Damion from making his final decision.

Aggie, Bob and I went to see Damion one more time. Once again, I saw that he was talking with the Blessed Mother. All he needed from his Earth mother was her unconditional love and permission for him to leave.

Damion passed over the next day. He walked into the Kingdom of the Angels, hand in hand with the Blessed Mother to meet his father on the other side.

Many times I've seen a loved one ready to depart, held back by the well-intentioned prayers of relatives. During each of my visits with Damion I was allowed to spend only a limited amount of time in his hospital room. However, if I had been an ordained minister I would have been able to stay longer with Damion to ease his way into the hereafter sooner.

In a very real sense, it was Damion who inspired my decision to become ordained.

25. LISTEN TO THE CHILDREN

*T*he insights from beyond that come to little children can be the most profound, joyful and fearless. I consider it a privilege to listen and talk to them.

My friend Joni has two grandchildren: Gianna and Vincent. One day, their mother, Jeannine, was holding Vincent, aged one, in her arms while Gianna, four years old, was walking alongside her. They were detained by a neighbor who wanted to chat briefly with Jeannine. Gianna knew that she wasn't allowed to cross the street by herself, but she was impatient about the delay and excited about visiting her grandparents. While Jeannine and the neighbor talked, Gianna decided that she would make the journey across the street on her own.

As she suddenly dashed across the street, she was hit by a car and tossed in the air. When her frantic mother reached her, Gianna was in shock, but she did not have a scratch on her body, nor did she suffer any broken bones. Taken to the doctor immediately, she kept repeating, "When I got hit by the car the angels caught me, that's why I wasn't hurt."

Gianna never mentioned the angels again until four years later when she and her brother Vincent were in the car with their grandfather. Their grandfather was parking his car and Vincent thought the car was stopped and pushed open the door to get out. Vincent's grandfather yelled at him for opening up the door and warned him he could get hurt.

"Vincent, you have to be careful," Gianna scolded her brother. "When I crossed the street by myself, I got hit by a car, but the angels caught me and that's why I didn't get hurt."

When Vincent was ten months old, his great-grandfather "Poppy" passed away. On the great-grandfather's anniversary, Vincent and his family would go to the grave to place flowers. On the way to the cemetery, their grandmother Joni explained to Vincent that Poppy was in heaven.

"No, he's not," Vincent replied. "He's not in heaven. He's in the attic."

"What does Poppy do in the attic?" Joni asked.

"He's watching over Great-grandma, so she doesn't fall and doesn't burn the pots."

"How do you know?" Joni asked.

"Because he told me," Vincent replied. "He laughs when I come up the stairs." Then Vincent went on to say, "Your uncle is in the attic, too. Poppy is with your uncle."

"Which uncle?" Joni asked.

"Great-grandma's brother," Vincent told her. "I don't know his name, but they are up there having a good time."

The message from the mouths of Joni's small grandchildren helped their great-grandmother believe in the ultimate reunion of loved ones.

The following story about an infant saved by an angel has an unusual twist. It comes from Pamela Penrose of Portland, Oregon, who describes her harrowing escape from death when she was four months old.

Seven-year-old Pamela Penrose, who lived with her parents and brothers and sisters in Artesia, California, crawled into her bed and pulled the blankets under her chin. As she cuddled against her pillow, she hoped that she would not have one of the frightening dreams that often woke her with a rapidly beating heart and a clutching fear that she would die. Often she threw her covers aside and bolted to the closet in her room and hid behind her clothes that hung from the pole suspended between the walls. There she would stay in the dark corner haunted by her nightmare and shivering with terror until she worked up the courage to run into the living room and switch on the TV. With the volume turned low, she watched the comforting images on the screen until she fell into exhausted sleep on the couch, or until morning light chased away the shadows.

One Friday night in May 1959, despite her vague apprehen-

sion about a nightmare visitation, Pamela fell into a deep, peace-
ful sleep until the image of herself as an infant cuddling in a
bassinet on the rear seat of her father's car came into her mind.
Usually, when a terrifying dream was taking shape in her consciousness, she would have a warning that it was going to be bad
and the warning was always accompanied by a desperate, sinking
feeling. But in her dreaming mind the picture of herself, a dark-
haired little baby with rosy cheeks, certainly no older than four
months, assured her that there was nothing to fear.

Even though her father was driving erratically and loudly
berating her mother—pounding her with his brutal voice and
drawing silent tears—the baby in the bassinet seemed undis-
turbed. There was no question in the portion of Pam's mind that
was monitoring her dream that the infant in the back seat was herself, seven years earlier. She thought it strange, though, that the
baby was not screaming with fright from her father's awful shout-
ing and maniacal driving. Now, suddenly, he whipped the steering
wheel in a sharp turn that drew screeching protest from the tires
as the car lurched to the right.

At that moment the right rear door, behind her mother's front
passenger seat, flew open and the infant Pam was wrenched from
her bassinet and hurled out the yawning door. For an instant,
Pam's mother turned in her seat and watched with horrified eyes
as her infant daughter flew from her safe perch on the back seat
through the open space of the flung-out door. Pam's tiny body
made an arc, then with a thump struck the hood of a truck trail-
ing slightly behind the Penrose's car in the outside right lane. After
striking the pickup, the baby's body disappeared, falling beneath
the speeding truck.

It was the terrible, crumpled expression on her mother's face
that touched seven-year-old Pam's heart as she saw her mother
dissolve into tears and shake as she screamed at her husband to
stop the car. It was in that same briefest of moments, after baby
Pam collided with the hood of the pickup, that the dreaming Pam
witnessed what she thought was a blue cloud of smoke appear in
the open rear door frame, then vanish like a sudden wind. She

would never forget, as the cloud passed, the sense of marvelous peace that stole through her body and imparted to her the unquestionable knowledge that baby Pam was safe, enfolded protectively in the arms of an angel.

Baby Pam was alive and safe. She did not die under the wheels of the pickup truck. Dreaming Pam knew, as a solemn, incontrovertible truth, that nothing would change. She as a baby had been saved from death by an angel. With a huge sigh and a warm feeling in her heart, Pam fell into a dreamless sleep.

It was at breakfast the next morning that Pam's mother made a startling announcement. Just the two of them, Pam and her mother Dione, sat across from each other at the table. Pam had already eaten her oatmeal and an orange, while her mother lingered over her coffee. From the moment she had seated herself after serving her daughter's breakfast, Dione had seemed strangely quiet, perturbed, with her brow wrinkled as if she were searching for the right words to convey a special thought. Finally, she said, "I think you are old enough for me to tell you about something that happened when you were a baby."

Pam looked at her mother sharply. What could her mother have to say to her that required a certain maturity on Pam's part to understand? She waited while her mother collected her thoughts and, choosing her words carefully, said, "When you were little, about four months old, you were in the car with your dad and me when he took a sharp turn. You flew out of your bassinet on the back seat and tumbled out of the rear door, which had popped open. It must not have been closed all the way.

"Anyway, you bounced off a pickup truck in the next lane and fell beneath the wheels. It all happened so fast that there was nothing I could do. I thought I'd go crazy. The truck passed over you. Your face was scraped but, miraculously, except for cuts on your face, you were not injured. The police came and called an ambulance. Doctors examined you at the hospital and everybody said it was a miracle you were alive. I thanked God for saving you. It was a miracle. Whenever you get sick or over-tired, you can see the tiny scars on your face."

Pam had been holding her tongue, incredulous that her mother somehow knew about her dream. She had not whispered a word about it. She never told her parents, or anybody, about any of her dreams. Even when they were horrible and frightening, she kept them to herself.

Furious with her mother, she shouted, "You're lying to me! Why would you lie to me?"

Dione Penrose sat back in her chair as if she had been struck by her daughter.

"Why would I lie to you?" she asked, leaning forward across the table and taking Pam's small hands in hers.

Confused, and ashamed that she had screamed at her mother, Pam mumbled, "I don't know. Why did you tell me now? I mean, why today?"

"I don't know," Dione said. "It just seemed like the proper time. I had no idea you'd be so upset."

Later, in her room, convinced that her mother's revelation was a strange coincidence, Pam suddenly felt a sense of deep peace settle over her and, although no voice came into her mind to explain the understanding that flowed into her like a soft and gentle whisper, she knew in her heart that the source of her wisdom was the same angelic visitor who had clasped her infant body in a protective embrace to save her life when she was four months old.

26. THE RAINBOW

A woman approached me at my lawyer's fiftieth birthday party. She asked me to do a reading for her.

"Here and now?" I said.

"Can you?" she replied.

"Sorry, but this is neither the time nor the place," I said, reluctantly.

The following afternoon Mike called me to say that his cousin Sue felt there must be something wrong because I would not tell her anything.

"She thinks that something bad is going to happen to her," Mike admitted.

"Not at all, Mike. Tell her to call my office so we can set up an appointment."

When it came time for Sue's appointment, she came in with a photo of a very pretty child.

"This is my friend's daughter. We were very close," she explained.

I could suddenly feel the side of my head pounding and a kind of swelling in my temple area.

"This child had a brain tumor," I told her.

I could feel the child standing next to me, then when her little spirit moved away so did the pain. I went on with the reading.

"I was hoping you could give me something tangible," she said.

I smiled. When her reading came to a close and she got up to leave, I felt compelled to say more.

"Can't you see the rainbow?" I asked her.

Sue turned back to me with tears running down her face.

"Those were the last words she spoke, before she closed her eyes and was gone," Sue explained.

27. THE SHAMAN OF PARK SLOPE

*L*ate in January 1993, I was to attend a meeting in the Park Slope area of Brooklyn. I had come to know by this time in my life that nothing is by chance. After the meeting, I walked along 7th Avenue and paused to look inside a bookstore window. I was suddenly filled with an uncomfortable sensation. I had the feeling I was being pulled inside. I decided to go with it and stepped into the shop, which was long and narrow. I could feel an energy pulling me toward the rear of the store. As much as I tried to resist it, I could not stop myself.

As I cautiously made my way toward the back of the store, I saw a woman crouching on the floor. My first impression was that she looked two thousand years old. As our eyes met, everyone in the store seemed to fall silent. I sensed all eyes were on us. I had the distinct sensation that I was experiencing everything in slow motion. The woman got up from the floor and put out her hand toward me.

"Tell me something," she said.

There was no way I could comply with what she asked. I glanced at her palms and saw in my mind's eye the crucifixion of Christ and the crown of the thorns resting on Jesus' head. I responded to her by telling her that she had been at the crucifixion and that I knew her from a previous lifetime. Then I gave her a message. I told her to pray to Saint Theresa. Everyone who was in the store let out a collective gasp.

A woman approached me and explained that Rosa, the proprietor, held healing circles in the rear of the bookstore.

"Rosa had told us that she would meet a man in three days' time who would give her the message of Saint Theresa," she said.

I was filled with a sense of healing, as though something wonderful had taken place between us. There were no other words spoken. I discovered later that Rosa was the resident psychic healer of Park Slope. I did not speak to her until days later when I went to her home to meet with her privately.

Rosa was a tiny woman, standing no more than four feet and eleven inches, with waist-length silky black hair and radiant dark eyes. I could sense in her a light of peace and harmony. Rosa told me that she was from Central America and that she was a shamanistic healer. She worked with snake medicine, which she described as an emotional detox transmutation. Her form of medicine/healing teaches people on a personal level that they are universal beings and can accept all aspects of life by shedding their fears and barriers. Rosa told me that I was very gifted, as well as a wonderful healer. I pondered the thought of being a healer for a few moments, then asked her, "Why?"

"Trust," she replied. "We are all born with the innate ability to heal, but first your fears must be shed as the snake sheds its skin. Once you shed the outer layers of fear and self-doubt, such as 'Can I?' and 'Am I really capable?' or the word 'Why?,' you experience trust for self."

Rosa invited me to stay for the evening's healing circle, and I was happy to accept her invitation. When everyone arrived, there were fifteen of us in the room. Rosa asked me if I minded if she worked on me, since it was my first time. I politely refused, and told her I would rather observe. A young woman then volunteered to go first. The young woman lay down on the floor and Rosa proceeded to burn sage to protect the place of ceremony. She began several prayers, followed by the burning of cedar so that the prayers were sure to rise up on the cedar smoke to the Creator.

When Rosa finished the ritual prayer, she placed her hands strategically on the young woman lying on the floor. Within moments the woman was crying. Rosa asked her to describe what she was feeling. She began telling us that she was feeling anger with her brother, an anger that had begun when she was eleven years old. As I looked at the young woman's face, I was struck by its sudden youthful, childlike quality. She seemed all of eleven years old. Rosa asked her why she was angry with her brother, then strangely asked someone to light a cigar for her. When this had been accomplished, Rosa took the smoke into her mouth, then cupped her hand and placed it over the woman's stomach. She released the smoke over the woman's abdomen. As Rosa blew the smoke the young woman suddenly declared, "He raped me!" Once this was out, she seemed to relax. With Rosa's help, the young woman shed a layer of pain she had carried for years, and would now be able to heal from within. The woman soon sat up and, even though she had been crying, I could see that there had been release of a long-carried burden.

Two months later I was to go again to one of Rosa's healing circles. It would prove to be unforgettable. We were about eleven people that night, and one woman stood out from the rest. She was behaving very strangely during the session. I will call her Sara. I managed to whisper to Rosa at one point that I felt this woman's energy was from the dark side.

"I'm not afraid of evil, are you?" she asked, chuckling.

"Rosa, you know I am." I wasn't afraid to admit it.

"Oh, you are a chicken," Rosa replied in her broken English.

Rosa asked Sara to sit in the center of the floor and positioned me behind her, sitting with what she called Archangel Michael's Sword of Protection. Rosa began to blow the smoke of the cigar over Sara's abdominal area. I suddenly felt what I was sure was a blue ray of lightning traveling up the handle of the sword. Then I felt it enter my hands. My body started to shake uncontrollably. Later, I was told my eyes had rolled back into my head and I had passed out. I was to lie on the floor for several minutes before I came to. In addition to that, everyone in the room had vomited.

To this surreal episode I would like to add a note of further explanation. Whenever an evil force becomes constellated in a person, if there is to be a healing it is best to include as many people in the healing as possible. The more people on the side of the light, the more diluted the darkness will become. I offer the flowing analogy. If a drop of black ink is added to a full pail of water, it will become more diluted than if it were only added to a small glass of water.

After the ritual had ended, I was struck by the difference in Sara's behavior. She seemed full of light.

28. TELL ME YOU LOVE ME

*T*here are many people who call me for phone readings because they cannot afford to travel to the New York area. Here is a story from a woman who reached me from California.

Lisa spoke with a French accent, and at first I couldn't understand her words on the phone because she was crying as if her heart were broken.

"My Francis died," she sobbed over and over.

I learned that Francis, her lover, had passed over during the night.

"Do you think you can reach him?" Lisa asked. "Or is it too soon?"

I asked Lisa to calm herself while I communicated with Francis. Summoning him was like picking up a telephone and dialing a number, because he answered me immediately.

"Lisa," I said after conversing with Francis, "Francis just told me that he passed over very quickly. He had a heart attack, and he did not bleed to death."

"When the paramedics picked up his body," Lisa exclaimed, "they told me they believed he bled to death after he fell. They told me he must have suffered for the remainder of the night."

"No," I said. "He explained to me that when he fell he hit his head on the floor. That is where all the blood came from."

Francis asked me to tell his grieving Lisa that even though he did not use the word "love" with her very often, he loved and cherished her very dearly.

"He said that he called you mon cherie."

"Is he angry with me?" Lisa asked. She was referring to an argument they had the night before he died, after which Francis returned to his own apartment. There he fell to the floor when he was struck by the heart seizure. The impact of the fall opened his head and he bled profusely. The two would not have had their disagreement, Lisa said, if only he had told her that he dearly loved her. I assured her that Francis was not angry with her, and gave her his request that she tell his family that he was with his grandmother. Francis then ended the communication as quickly as it had begun.

Lisa called me a few weeks later to inform me that an autopsy revealed that Francis had certainly died from a heart attack, and that he had not bled to death. She was relieved that his passing had occurred quickly, with little pain. She thanked me for restoring her peace of mind and convincing her, through Francis, that he loved her with all his heart.

29. THE LAST DANCE

I received a call early one morning. "I am so sorry to bother you at eight in the morning," the woman said. "My name is Roe; I got your number from my friend Betty, who came to you for a reading."

As my caller rambled on, I had to tell her to slow down.

Making a deliberate attempt to be more collected, Roe said, "I need to know that he is all right. He died from AIDS."

"Roe, who passed over?" I asked.

"My brother," she answered.

"Are you saying that you are afraid he did not make it to God's White Light because he died from this particular disease?"

"Well, yes," was Roe's reply. "Can you help me? I need to know that Tom's okay."

"Roe," I began, "although he lived a different lifestyle, that doesn't mean he didn't pass over into the heavenly realm."

I asked Roe to hold on one moment while I communicated with Tom.

"Roe, your brother tells me that he danced his way to the other side. He is showing me a pair of tap shoes, and tells me that you and he were a dance team when you were younger." I could hear her crying. "Tom says that you do not have to worry about him," I went on. "He is out of pain. And when it's your time to pass over, he will be waiting for one last dance."

She was sobbing after hearing her brother's assurances from me. I waited for her to calm down before I continued, "Your brother would like to thank you for being there and making his last days on the Earth plane comfortable."

I was never able to meet Roe in person.

30. MISSING

*M*y friend Steve and I were working together on a children's spiritual book. After he'd been with me for about an hour, he asked if he could use my telephone to call his mother who lived in another state. He had been unable to reach his family for the past two days.

After he dialed, I heard him say, "Oh, hi, Uncle Gary. Where have you been for the past couple of days?" To his uncle's reply, I heard Steve say, "Does anyone know where he is?" Then he asked to speak with his mother. After a few minutes I heard him exclaim, "Oh mama, that's terrible." When Steve completed his phone call, my curiosity was aroused. He told me that a friend of his family, Ron, was missing and Steve's mother was greatly concerned because he had left a suitcase, presumably with clothes in it, in Steve's mother's garage, with her permission.

Immediately I had a vision of the missing man, who was wearing a plaid shirt and brown pants. Next, I saw a car that appeared to be parked near two tall oil rigs and an adjacent body of water. I warned Steve that I saw drugs in Ron's suitcase that he had left behind.

"What do you think happened to Ron?" Steve asked.

"I believe this man was murdered," I said.

At this point, Steve asked if I would mind if he used my phone again. "I need to call my mother back," he said.

Steve asked his mother whether Ron had been wearing a plaid shirt and brown pants when he disappeared. His mother verified the accuracy of my impression about Ron's clothes, and told her son that a few days before Ron was presumed missing, he had returned long enough to retrieve the suitcase from the garage.

"Was his car found in an area near oil wells?" Steve asked.

"Yes," she answered.

"Mama, he said, "do you know that he might have had drugs in that suitcase?"

"Do you think that if I had known there were drugs in the suitcase I would have given him permission to leave it here?"

A few days later, she called Steve to tell him that the police believed drugs certainly were a probable factor in Ron's disappearance. Unfortunately, five years after Steve learned about his missing friend, Ron still had not communicated with either Steve or his mother.

31. JOY THROUGH TEARS

*T*he client/healer relationship is a sacred one. The relationship itself can take many forms and the dynamic is always unique and ever-changing. But what doesn't change is the responsibility I feel toward my client's well-being. As I am frequently a messenger, there are times when the spirit will show me information but won't wish me to share it with the client at the present moment. It becomes my duty to uphold the integrity of the proceedings and to behave responsibly, even in the face of a client eager to know all. Still, being human, the tears my clients shed have often been mirrored by my own.

One day I stopped into the drugstore to pick up a prescription. Charlie smiled from behind the counter.

"Hey, Ed, how's it going? I'm glad you stopped in. I need directions from you to get to a party on Staten Island this Saturday night," Charlie said.

"What's the name of the street you're going to?" I asked, glad to oblige him.

"I don't have it with me, but I'll bring it tomorrow."

"Fine. I'll stop by sometime in the afternoon and give you the directions," I promised.

The following afternoon I went back to the drugstore. Charlie had the street address as he told me he would. I looked at the address which was written on a small piece of paper, then I looked up at Charlie. Before I gave him the directions I asked him how he was feeling.

"Great. I just came back from a vacation with my wife. When I got back I saw the doctor and got a full checkup. Why do you ask?" he said with a slight apprehension in his voice. I told him I was just making conversation. As I went on to give him the directions, my mind was saying, Charlie, you are never going to this party. You're going to be dead by Friday night.

Charlie told me how much he was looking forward to seeing the people who were sure to be there. "I haven't seen some of them in years," he exclaimed.

"Charlie," I ventured, "You look a bit tired. Why don't you see your doctor?"

"I told you, I just had a checkup. The doctor said I was fine. I just didn't sleep well last night."

I smiled and wished him luck on his journey. He looked at me rather strangely and reminded me that he was only going from Long Island to Staten Island. That Saturday I heard Charlie had passed away in his sleep.

32. DENIAL

*M*y son Phil asked if I would do a reading for his chiropractor. The woman's father had passed away one year before. As the doctor sat before me, I could detect she was having difficulty accepting what I was telling her. Several times throughout the session she told me, "I'm sorry. You are wrong." When I was assured of her father's vibrations, I informed her that her father was telling me his estate remained unsettled. She looked at me with even more doubt. "You're wrong," she said, "I took care of all my father's affairs myself." I told her that he was telling me that in a week's time his affairs would finally be in order.

After I finished the reading, I allowed my ego to get in the way. Instead of trusting the universe that I had heard what I heard and had passed on the correct information, I doubted myself. I became preoccupied with concern for my son, thinking I had failed him somehow. A week later, I learned that the chiropractor had gotten in touch with Phil, anxious to apologize to me. "Everything that your father said was true," she conceded. "I was so taken aback that he was giving me a message from the other side, I went into a kind of denial. I needed to have some time to let it all register in my mind. I received a call from the insurance company this morning telling me that my father's premium was late."

She confessed to Phil that she had been completely unaware of this particular insurance policy. Now her father's affairs would finally be in order.

33 · BIG AUNT LOUISE

A wonderful spirit came pushing into a session I was having with a woman named Louise. At first I could feel that it was a man's vibration, and then I saw him tip his hat to Louise, which made me smile. I was about to relay this when suddenly a female presence emerged, pushing the male aside as if she was determined to go first. As the woman spoke, I relayed her message to Louise. "This woman says she's bossy and loves parties and that she intends to stick around the entire evening!"

Louise laughed hysterically and explained, "It's my big aunt Louise!"

Aunt Louise was wearing a beautiful turquoise gown. "I know exactly which gown you mean," Louise confirmed. "It was a gown she wore once to a family wedding."

Aunt Louise told me to tell Louise that her sisters and brothers always treated her like she was their mother. Louise began to laugh and cry at the same time. At that moment, Louise's niece, Roe, entered the room.

I told Roe, "Your aunt tells me that you used to tease her about the few whiskers she had on her chin."

Roe confessed this was so.

"I always teased her," Roe replied, "and then I tweezed her."

34. THE PHOTOGRAPH

*A*n appointment was scheduled for a woman named Debbie. As soon as Debbie sat down, she told me that her only question was in regard to her sister.

"I am not here about love, money or my own personal problems. I'm only here to find out about my sister," she stated directly.

Debbie had brought along two photographs, one of her sister and one of someone else. She handed me the photograph of her sister.

"Your sister tells me she worked with the elderly. I see two cars . . . and I hear a train," I told her.

"Ed, can you tell me where my sister is?" Debbie said bluntly.

"Debbie, your sister is on the other side," I said.

"Can you tell me anything else?"

"She's telling me that her purse and keys were left in the car," I replied.

Debbie had began to tell me exactly what had happened. Two years before, her sister had left work, got into her car, and been followed by another car. No one had seen or heard from her since.

"Before I came here, I knew my sister was dead," Debbie confessed. She handed me the other photograph. "He killed her, didn't he?" she said, more like a statement of fact than a question.

I looked down at the photograph, gazed into the man's eyes, then back into Debbie's eyes. I hesitated for a moment.

"You know, don't you?" she said.

Like Debbie, I was certain this man had killed her sister. Knowledge can be a burden when the truth is not attractive. My life has caused me to bear witness to many such harsh truths, as well as affording me visions of the truly miraculous and sublime.

35 . BEST FRIENDS

A twenty-one-year-old woman came to me for a reading. "Chris," I said. "You need to let go of your pain. You are letting go of everything around you, instead of what's truly going on inside you. You need to heal yourself."

The name Annie came through from the other side. I looked at Chris and told her, "Before I continue, do you understand the work that I do? I communicate with loved ones who have crossed over." After I explained further, I asked her if she wanted me to continue. She said she did.

"Chris, your friend Annie was in a car accident," I said.

"That's how she died," Chris explained.

"Annie asked me to mention a name. Joey. Something about five years ago . . . and a heart-shaped pendant," I added.

"I went out with a boy named Joey five years ago," she responded, "and he gave me a heart-shaped pendant. What does he have to do with Annie and me?"

"Annie wanted you to know that she is always around you. You shared many teenage secrets. Annie is telling me that you have to let go of the pain of losing her," I instructed.

"I just can't forget her," Chris said with a confused urgency.

"Chris, she does not want you to forget her. She wants you to start having fun in your life."

Chris looked at me with tears in her eyes.

"But she was my best friend."

"Annie says you mailed her a little stuffed animal for her last birthday," I revealed.

"That's right," Chris agreed.

When the session was complete, Chris giggled through the tears.

"Gee, that was like having a long-distance phone call without the toll charges."

36. THE LAST PHOTO

A very good friend of mine asked if I could make time that same day to see someone as soon as possible. Knowing my friend to be someone who would not ask for anything that wasn't truly needed, I agreed to see this person later that day.

I went to the client's home, and a young, very teary-eyed woman named Nina met me at the door. Her fiancé, Bill, had broken up with her two days prior. I asked Nina if she had a photograph of her fiancé. She went into another room and came out minutes later with twenty photographs in her hand. She handed me Bill's photograph first and I proceeded to tell her that the man was presently seeing someone else, but that he would realize he had made a drastic mistake.

"He's going to come back into your life," I told her.

She then showed me a photograph of her father.

"Nina, I'm very sorry to tell you this, but your father was an alcoholic," I said.

"My father is deceased."

"Your father is also telling me that when he drank . . . you would hide under the basement stairway so that he would not abuse you. He says he's very sorry for that."

When the session was complete and I was just about to leave, Nina said, "Could you look at just one more picture? I would like to know something about my friend."

Nina went back into the other room and came out with yet another photograph and handed it to me. As I looked at the picture, I felt my head being pulled back and I began to lose my breath. I was actually gasping for air and felt a sharp pain go through my chest. As I tried to recover myself, Nina became frantic and kept telling me over and over she was sorry.

"I couldn't believe what you were telling me, so I decided to test you," she confessed. "Steve was killed three years ago with a knife wound to the chest."

37. JACK OF SPADES

*L*orraine is a person who helps everyone. A stranger in the street could ask her for her coat and Lorraine would hand it to him and say thank you. I received a call from her one afternoon and listened as she talked non-stop about a friend who needed to see me at once but could not afford to pay me. Her friend, Theresa, was concerned about a lump on her breast. Could I please see her that night? I agreed to meet Theresa later that evening.

On meeting Theresa, she told me that her doctor had advised her she would need immediate surgery to remove the lump. I handed her a deck of playing cards, and I told her to shuffle the deck. As she was shuffling the cards, the jack of spades slipped out and slid across the table.

"You're separated," I said rather cryptically.

"Yes, I am," she replied.

This seemed to give her some comfort in my ability. Moments later I could hear Theresa's grandmother telling me how she got the lump on her breast. The young woman's husband had hit her with a chair, resulting in a swelling the size of a small tangerine. I repeated to Theresa what her grandmother had said. She looked down in shame and admitted it was true; her husband had hit her with a chair. Still, she could not be certain this had caused the lump. I asked her to put her hand on her breast so I could rest my hand on hers in order to feel the lump myself.

"Will I have to have a mastectomy? Do I have cancer? I don't want to have the surgery," she said.

"Theresa, you don't have cancer." I assured her.

I proceeded to tell her that it was important for her to take her doctor's advice. She continued to express her worst fear, certain that the doctor was going to have to remove her breast. She began to cry. Once again I assured her that it was not going to be necessary for her to have a mastectomy. "I promise you that you will walk out of the hospital with both your breasts," I told her. Three days later, Lorraine called me right after the surgery to tell me the lump had not been cancerous and that it had in all likelihood been caused by some kind of physical trauma.

38. THE GRANDMOTHERS

I was asked to bring forth spirit for three women. As I sat looking at their three different faces, I felt their anxiety as they awaited their messages from a loved one. I first spoke to Lisa because her grandmother had come forward and given me a very profound message to be passed along to Lisa's mother. I proceeded to tell her that her grandmother wished her to tell her mother that she was sorry for all the wrongs she had put her mother through while she was on the Earth plane. The grandmother had made it clear to me that she was proud of the person Lisa's mother had become. She was sorry for not having shown her how dearly she loved her daughter.

I have found it a common occurrence for loved ones to come forward with a need to address the pain they have inflicted, that they might make good what wrongs they had done during their lives. Lisa's mother called me the next day to thank me for sending this message, and to confirm that what her mother had said had reflected the facts of their lives together.

Meanwhile, Joanne and her sister Linda waited anxiously to hear what their grandmother might have to say. Their beloved grandmother had passed over four months earlier. When I finally felt her presence, she spoke of giving each of the girls something special. I could feel my ring finger twitch, indicating that one had been given a ring, yet something told me there was a missing element. I looked at Joanne and said, "Your grandmother gave you a ring, but I feel there's something missing." Joanne confirmed that she had been given her grandmother's engagement ring and that the diamond had fallen out. She proceeded to confess she had been concerned for the last seven months about her career, as she had been unemployed and looking for work. I could distinctly hear her grandmother tell me that Joanne would get a new job roughly three months from our meeting. She was eventually able to replace the missing diamond.

Linda's message started out strangely. "Linda, you stole my bracelet." Yet for all intents and purposes Linda seemed overjoyed at these words. When her combination of laughter and tears subsided and she calmed down, the truth became clear. Linda explained that her grandmother had given her a bracelet long before she had passed over and often lovingly teased her that she had stolen it.

39 · BERNICE'S PIANO

*J*im was one of the people who climbed Mount Sinai with me. He is a wonderfully energetic senior citizen. I had watched this determined man climb with courage, strength and fortitude, ever moving toward the top of the mountain. Jim told me, "I need to do this just like Moses did thousands of years ago."

Jim asked me if I would do a reading for him. When Jim's sister Bernice came forth, I could see her standing near a grand piano. "Bernice tells me she was a professional singer when she was on the Earth plane, and loved to travel." Jim assured me this was correct. I proceeded to tell Jim that Bernice wanted him to know that it was time to let go, particularly in regard to the piano. She wanted him to sell it and with the proceeds go on a wonderful cruise. Jim said that he had been debating whether to let the piano go. I informed him, "Bernice wants you to go on a cruise like the one she went on, when she brought you back the Delft dish." I told him that he needn't worry, he would always feel her vibrations around even after the piano was gone.

Jim sold the piano and went on several marvelous cruises. He felt that even though he could have afforded to go even if he hadn't sold the piano, it had been important to let go and get on with his life. With the love he felt in his heart for his sister, the cruises were all the more wonderful.

40. DEVOTION

*M*rs. T came to see me hoping to communicate with her daughter Lilly, who had passed on several months prior. Lilly thanked her mother for the roses, but asked her if she would give them in the name of the Blessed Mother because the offering of roses should be offered to Our Lady. Mrs. T told me that Lilly was devoted to the Blessed Mother. Before her daughter had passed over, she had made up over a hundred pamphlets on the apparitions of Our Lady, but was never able to mail them out.

Lilly spoke of herself in ways that clearly showed she had lived a life of order. As I spoke with Mrs. T, my right hand suddenly went involuntarily toward my left shoulder as if something was disturbing me. Mrs. T began to cry. She told me this is what her daughter had done in her final days. She would tug on the tube that was connected to the left side of her body.

Lilly spoke of her mother's disappointment over some of the unloving members of the family. Lilly wanted her mother to know that the most important thing was the love of children for their mother, and that she indeed loved her mother very much. Lilly also asked me to relay that in the heavenly realm, Lilly was happily surrounded by children.

41. GRANDMOTHER'S RING

*D*onna was so anxious that she came to her appointment a half hour early, as did her grandmother who had passed over five years before. Donna became teary-eyed when I told her that her grandmother was present.

Donna's grandmother spoke of a diamond wedding ring she had left to her. "I don't have any wedding ring of my grandmother's," Donna corrected.

"The grandmother's last request was for your mother to give you that ring," I explained.

"I believe you. My mother, however, never told me about the ring. She'll probably never give it to me," Donna declared.

"Donna, don't be negative. Always be positive in everything you do," I advised her.

A few weeks later, I met Donna in a doctor's office. As soon as she saw me she held out her hand, overjoyed. On her finger was her grandmother's ring.

"Ed," Donna said, "I asked my mother about the ring and she told me she didn't think I'd want to have it."

She went on to tell me that she had not gotten the chance to say goodbye to her grandmother before she passed over. With the ring on her finger, she said she felt closer to her grandmother. I told her that our loved ones are always with us, even if we can't see them with our eyes.

42. THE DOCTOR'S OFFICE

I have little patience for sitting in a doctor's office. I have often put off going, even when I knew it was necessary that I do so. One particular afternoon was no exception. It was flu season, and I was debating about putting off my appointment yet another week. I called the doctor's office to find out how long the wait would be. The nurse told me to come right over, as there was no one in the waiting room at the moment. I hurried over and arrived within a few minutes of my call. In the interim, a gentleman had come in and was talking to a nurse. He appeared to be in his late sixties, and he glanced over at me when I came in. He was speaking to the nurse about his son, telling a story that had happened when the boy was three years old. Because of this simple detail, I found myself listening more intently.

He explained that his son was afraid of the dark, and each night he asked that the light in his bedroom be kept on. The man's wife felt that this was simply a habit that needed to be broken. One night, the man went into the boy's room and told him that there was nothing to fear. He explained that God and the angels would look after him during the day and the night. The boy seemed to accept what his father was saying, and told him that it was okay to turn the light out. The father left the boy's bedroom, pleased that he had been able to impart a few words that would take the boy's fears away. When he got back to bed, where his wife lay waiting, she immediately asked him if he had spoken with Joseph.

"Yes," he told her, "and I shut off the light."

"I'm not sure that what you told him really worked," she responded.

"Why?" he asked her.

She pointed to the light shining beneath their son's door. The father got out of bed and headed back to his son's room. As he got closer to Joseph's door, he could hear the boy talking out loud. He opened the door and was nearly blinded by a bright light hovering at the foot of the child's bed. In the middle of the light was a winged angel holding a caduceus (the rod with two snakes winding around it that is used as a symbol of medicine). Joseph looked up at his father and said, "Daddy, this is my guardian angel."

The man told us that his son became a doctor when he grew up. As I continued to wait for my flu shot, I wondered, had the angel holding up the caduceus shown the boy his destiny?

43. FAMILY FOREVER

*J*oann came to me with great concerns about her health. Two months earlier her doctor had discovered a lump in her left breast during a routine examination. The doctor told her that it wasn't necessarily cancerous, and that the outcome did not have to be that of her sister, who had died of breast cancer. Only the tests would tell. Later that night, Joann sat in her bedroom crying, trying to decide how to tell her husband and children. Recalling how hard it had been for her sister's children, she remembered that her sister Pat had never given up. Pat's faith in God had given her the strength to go on with whatever life had in store. Joann wondered if she possessed the same strength.

One afternoon, while lying on her bed, Joann suddenly felt a presence in the room. She turned to see Pat standing by the bed, and froze in fear. Pat smiled and Joann marveled at how youthful and serene she looked. Joann's fear quickly melted away as she listened to her sister's familiar voice. "There is nothing for you to worry about," she told Joann. Before Joann could regain her composure enough to say, "I miss you," Pat was gone.

Two weeks later, Joann was in the doctor's office awaiting the results of her tests. Her fear was mounting, even though she tried to turn her thoughts to her sister's words and take comfort in them. When the doctor finally spoke to her, his first words were, "You have nothing to worry about." With tears running down her face, Joann told the doctor that his words echoed those said by her sister just two weeks before. The doctor was perplexed because he knew that Pat had died five years earlier.

Family members like Pat remain close to their loved ones after death, and I have often observed this bond extended to new family members whom the person never met in life. Such was the case with my client Gloria.

On the morning of her wedding, Gloria awoke with a start.

Standing in front of her was a strange man. She screamed and asked him, "What do you want?" The man vanished. Gloria's mom raced into the room to see why her daughter had screamed. "Gloria, what's the matter?" she asked.

In a shaken voice, Gloria responded, "Ever since I was a little girl I have felt a presence around me. Just now I could see him standing right in front of me."

Gloria's mother asked her to describe the man. She told her mother that he had a kind, loving smile, and that he wore a plaid shirt, black pants, and a tan baseball cap.

"With," her mother added, "a red feather."

Gloria was incredulous. "How did you know that, Mom?" she asked.

Her mother sat down on the bed. "That's what your father was wearing the day he died."

In fact, Gloria had never met her father in life as he had passed away prior to her birth.

44. THE LADY IN BLUE

*N*atalie's mother had been in the hospital for two months. During one of her daily visits, Natalie noticed a woman standing at her mother's bedside in a tailored blue suit. When Natalie came into the room, the woman discreetly left. Something about the lady gave Natalie a sense of inner peace. No words had been exchanged, but the lady's kind smile expressed the universal language of love and kindness. The next day, when Natalie returned, she again saw the lady in the blue suit and once again they exchanged warm smiles. Natalie did not ask her mother who the lady was. She decided to ask the lady herself the next time she saw her.

The very next day, Natalie arrived to find the lady in blue at her mother's bedside, and this time she could hear the two of them talking. She strained to hear what the lady was saying to her mother: "Margie, you have helped so many people in your life. There is no need to have fear." Natalie could see her mother smiling at the lady from her pillow. Natalie made her way into the room and approached the lady, asking her who she was. She thought the lady's face appeared to glow. The lady only responded with, "I'll be back in three hours." Then she left the room. Natalie asked her mother to identify the lady, but she only smiled.

Three hours later, when it was time for the lady to return, Natalie's mother passed over. Natalie stood at her mother's bedside, weeping. Through her tears she saw the lady in blue enter the room. "Don't cry, Natalie," the lady told her. "Your mother is fine. She loved and helped so many people. That is why I came to her bedside." There was a wonderful smile on her face as she spoke. When Natalie again asked for her name, the lady replied, "Mary." At that moment, a friend of Natalie's walked into the room. When Natalie turned to introduce her friend to Mary, the lady was gone.

Two weeks later, Natalie went back to the hospital in hopes of finding Mary. No staff member knew of a Mary who worked for the hospital, nor had they ever seen a Mary who had visited with her mother.

45. DREAMS

*S*ome dreams may have great significance for the dreamer. There are dreams that can be paranormal involving clairvoyance, telepathy or precognition. In ancient times, dreams were seen as supernatural events bearing prophesies, predictions, and messages from God.

I rarely recall my own dreams unless they are going to have some form of significance for me. After many years of appearing on the hallway landing, my great-grandma Lily came to me for the first time in a dream. She didn't speak but only smiled, her arms folded just as they were in the visions I had seen of her so many times before. When I awoke from the dream, I thought it was strange. I had never dreamed of her before. Later that same day my beloved grandmother was to join her own mother in heaven.

I have been asked many times to interpret dreams. One such request came from a woman who had been very close to her grandmother who had passed over a few years before. She told me that in her dream her grandmother was standing on a large rock surrounded by turbulent black water. She was black as well, and held in her hand a black handkerchief. The wind was so strong it was trying to pull the handkerchief from her hand. I suggested that her grandmother was letting her know she was waiting for her husband, being that she was "dressed in black." When the time came for him to cross over, there would be major difficulties within the family over money and property, thus "the wind trying to take her handkerchief." I explained that her grandmother was warning her to stand strong in the aftermath of her grandfather's passing. That was why she was "standing on the rock." The dark murky water signified trouble for the dreamer.

Within a week's time, her dream seemed to come to fruition. There were indeed numerous fights over money. The young woman stood firm no matter how hard her family pushed her. Armed with the information of a single dream, the woman would successfully receive what her grandparents had left her.

I call the following dream an "open eye dream," while some may call this a vision into the near future. I was standing in front of my place of business taking in the freshness of a wonderful spring day, preoccupied with my inner thoughts. I turned to look to the left and saw one of my neighbors, George, getting out of his car. As I watched George walk toward the entrance of his store, I could see his ethereal body (his life force) hovering a few feet above the ground, as though out of sync with his physical body. He looked as if he were walking on air. I wondered about the separation. I considered going over to him and asking him if he was having any problems that I might be able to help him with. Unfortunately, I was called back into my store for a phone call.

The following afternoon I was visited by one of the local police officers in the area. He informed me that George had committed suicide the preceding night. My eyes welled up with tears. Could I have reached out to help him through whatever difficult time he was having? Had my vision been a call to action?

46. THE INSTITUTE OF CREATIVE HEALING

few years ago, a friend introduced me to Helene, the founder of the Institute of Creative Healing, an organization that led me further down my life path.

I donate two nights a month to the groups that attend the Institute of Creative Healing. There are several groups within the Institute, including those for psychic development, yoga, meditation, and bereavement. The most difficult, yet most rewarding work I do at the Institute is with the bereavement group, a gathering of people who are interested in peeking beyond the veil to communicate with loved ones.

Not long after I met Helene, she invited me to be the evening keynote speaker for a bereavement group. Most of the members of the group had lost children, husbands or wives. When I arrived, there were approximately thirty people in the room. As I looked at each person's face, I murmured the Lord's Prayer and asked God for the strength to give each of them exactly what he or she needed to hear. I also asked God to banish my old fears so that I could work freely. I remembered the priest who told me that my gift of sight came from God. That night, as I brought forth each person's loved one, there were tears of joy and sadness.

One of the members with whom I worked in this group was named Ed. Before I began, Ed asked to speak with me for a moment alone.

He said, "I need to tell you that I am not a believer."

"That is fine," I responded. "I am not here to make you a believer." I thanked him for his honesty.

As we entered the room, I looked at the other faces. I wondered if I could help them. I took in three deep breaths and put aside my fears. Then I spoke to each person individually. When I came to Ed, the non-believer, I stopped for a moment and said,

"Your daughter tells me that she is always around you. She hands you a rose every day. She is wearing a green dress."

"I don't know what that means," Ed answered.

At the end of the evening, Ed thanked me courteously and said, "The others seemed to be quite impressed. But I don't understand what you meant."

"I think in time you will understand," I assured him.

The next day I received a call from Helene, the woman who had invited me to the center. After she greeted me, she said, "Ed told you that he didn't know what the rose and the green dress meant. But he called, excited and eager to see you again, because he remembered that in the hallway of his home there is a picture on the wall of his daughter in a green dress holding a single rose." On my next visit to the center, Ed's daughter came forth once again, but out of respect for Ed's privacy, I cannot reveal the information that was given.

Another client I worked with was Marsha, a sweet senior citizen. Marsha's vibrations could light up a room. She is always eager to help and learn. As I worked with Marsha, her husband, who had passed over seventeen years earlier, came through to speak to her. Strangely, he showed me a pair of old shoes. As I relayed this image, the look on Marsha's face was one of confusion. After a moment of thought she explained that her husband only bought secondhand shoes.

Marsha's husband went on to tell me that there were three celebrations coming up all in the same day. Marsha smiled. "Yes, there are," she answered. "My husband's birthday and our anniversary."

I smiled and felt warmed, knowing in advance the nature of the third celebration.

"And the day we first met," Marsha said. "They all come on the same day."

"Your husband tells me that you both loved to dance," I told Marsha.

"Yes we did," she replied. "And I miss him so dearly."

Marsha was pleased with the messages from her husband. She

told me that it gave her peace of mind to know that in some form she could still communicate with him. Whenever I've seen Marsha since our first meeting, I see a pair of dancing shoes in my mind's eye and that is how I know that her husband is with us.

I met a woman and her daughter Nancy at the center. They came to see me two months after a tragic loss. The mother was in such pain that I held her hand to comfort her. Then I asked her other daughter, who had passed over, to come forward.

"Your daughter tells you not to feel guilty," I began.

"I do feel guilty," she admitted.

"You did not give her the cancer that she died from," I told her.

Nancy, who sat next to her mother, told me some of the details of her sister's illness and death. I turned to Nancy and said, "Your sister has shown me a scapular (a small picture of a saint). You took it from her the day she passed over."

Nancy asked if her sister was upset that she had taken the scapular.

"No, she is not angry with you," I responded. Then I asked, "Why did you give the scapular to your aunt?"

"I gave it to my aunt because she was very sick," Nancy said. "However, from the moment I gave it to her, I wanted to ask for it back, but I felt too guilty to do it."

"Nancy," I went on. "Your sister said she knows you have a very big heart, but she would like you to have the scapular."

"Do you think I could ask my aunt for it?" Nancy asked.

"Your sister is telling you to ask for it back. She assures me that your aunt will not be angry."

I saw Nancy about two weeks later. She was pleased to show me that she was wearing the scapular and told me that her aunt had been happy to return it. Nancy thanked me again for the communication with her sister, and told me that her mother's conscience was eased.

Petrina was another member of the bereavement group. When it was her turn for her loved one to come forth, I received a message from her son, Freddie. He told me that his mother was a very private person, so I asked her if she would mind meeting at the end of the evening. Then I could deliver her message without others present. She agreed.

At the end of the evening, Petrina's message was a kiss and a hug from Freddie. Petrina cried and asked if she could meet with me alone. I agreed.

When I arrived at Petrina's home, the lights blinked. Petrina explained that every time she felt her son's presence they would blink. I could see Freddie standing by the kitchen sink. During his life, this was the place where he and his mother often had their conversations. The most important message Freddie had for his parents was love. I gave his words to his mother: "It is now time for you to enjoy your life. Life should be lived and enjoyed to the fullest, and sorrow is yesterday's news." As I related his last words, tears ran down Petrina's face.

"I know that is what my son, Freddie, would want," she told me. "I just can't let go."

When I met his sister, Deena, Freddie told me how he regretted missing a dance with her at her wedding. They had been scheduled to dance to the song "My Way." Deena told me that she had intended to instruct the band to play "My Way" as the last song of the night, but with all of the excitement of the day's festivities, she simply forgot.

Claudia was another woman in the bereavement group. She was struggling to cope with losing her father, Louis, and came to me hoping to receive messages from him. Her father came through with ease.

One of his first messages was, "Don't fence with things."

"That was one of my father's favorite expressions," Claudia told me.

"Your father wants me to tell you that he loves the other side so much, it's better than the daily double." Claudia explained that this was another one of his famous expressions. Claudia then asked about her mother. From the way she posed her question, I thought that her mother was in the spirit world. However, as I reached into the spirit world I could not find her.

"Your mother has not passed over," I told Claudia.

"You're right, my mother is not dead," she replied. "I want to know if my father has a message for her." Louis talked about his missing medal and mentioned that Claudia's mother was always misplacing things. Claudia chuckled. Then my hands began to shake. As Claudia noticed this, she explained that her father had Parkinson's disease and that his hands used to shake, just like mine.

"Sometimes my physical body takes on the characteristics of the loved one I am working with," I explained to Claudia. "Your father mentions papers that will be coming to you," I told Claudia. "He tells me that the papers won't be pleasant and you will be going to court."

"Yes, I am waiting for papers to come in the mail," she responded.

"He tells me it will be a slow process, but all will be fine in the end," I assured her.

Louis also told her not to worry about the finances of the business and that she should play more and worry less. Claudia has since sent me many people who wish to make contact with departed loved ones.

A sweet-looking woman, twenty-one years old, sat within the bereavement group one evening. She wanted to speak with her brother who had passed away. As her brother came forth, I could feel a tremendous pressure on the side of my head, and I realized that her brother had been shot.

"Your brother tells me that he is not angry at your choice," I said to her.

She looked at me with tears in her eyes, and I noticed that she was nervous about what I revealed in front of the group. It was clear that she was reticent about revealing certain personal facts. Her brother knew what was meant by the "choice" she had made. She had chosen a gay sexual orientation and wanted her dead brother's approval. I began to speak to the young woman in a very gentle voice, "Your brother is not judging you. Are you judging yourself?

"Maybe," was her answer.

"If you judge yourself, then how can you expect others not to judge you? All your brother would like is for you to be happy."

She asked again if her brother was certain about his approval.

"Absolutely," was the reply I gave her from him.

"If my brother were still alive he would have judged me harshly," she explained.

Sometimes, when I am working with someone in a group and their loved one gives me a personal message, I try to word it such in a way that only the person in the audience for which it is intended can understand. If she misses the full meaning of the message, I tell her that I will speak to her privately.

I met AnnMarie and Larry at the center eight months after their son Larry, Jr. died. The first time I communicated with the younger Larry, I couldn't understand why he would only speak in half sentences, dance away, and return a moment or two later to complete the second half of the sentence. As he relayed his messages in this manner, I said to his parents, "I can't understand why he starts to give me a message, goes away for a bit, and then comes back to finish."

They explained that this was exactly what their son had done while he was on the Earth plane. "He was always on the move, doing three and four things at once. He never sat still," his mother explained. "He was eighteen years old. Even when there was nothing going on he always had something to do."

One message from Larry was quite sentimental and touching. It came through just before Christmas 1996, and young Larry told me that he intended to leave a rocking horse Christmas ornament under the tree as a gift for his mother. After the holidays, I talked to Larry, Sr. and AnnMarie and they informed me with happy tears in their eyes that, indeed, under the tree on Christmas Eve they had found a rocking horse ornament that seemed to have fallen off the tree.

"Larry, Jr. tells me that he loved angel food cake," I told AnnMarie.

"Yes," she replied. "Little Larry loved angel food cake."

"This one will have chocolate icing," I told her.

"Well, he certainly loved angel food cake," she explained, "but not with chocolate icing."

On the one-year anniversary of Larry, Jr.'s passing, I attended a Mass held in his memory. The church was filled to capacity, and there was not even room to stand. It seemed as if Larry had written the Mass himself, including little jokes and wonderful memories sprinkled throughout the service. I believe that he wanted to be remembered by everyone, even those like myself who didn't know him well, and he communicated with us from the other side with joyful laughter.

The next day, one of AnnMarie's co-workers brought in a cake, placed it on her desk and announced, "It's an angel food cake." When the box was opened, AnnMarie looked at the chocolate icing with wide eyes and recalled what her son had predicted about the icing in a message to me several months earlier. It was as if Larry, Jr. was thanking his mother for the wonderful memorial service.

When I relay a message from the spirit world, it does not necessarily mean that the message will come true that day or that month. It may even take years.

Little Larry's father told me, "It's strange that with all the pain we have been through with the loss of our son, I believe more in God now than I ever have. If you could only see the people's faces as you are delivering messages to each person. The smiles and tears reflect an overwhelming gratefulness to have those precious communications."

As I was working with a woman named Tina, her daughter, who had died more than two years earlier, came forth.

"Your daughter tells me how difficult it has been on you since her passing," I told Tina. "She wants you to know she is fine. She wants me to tell you that you should start enjoying your life. Tina, she hands you a bouquet of roses and wishes you a happy birthday."

With tears running down her face, Tina said, "Today is my birthday."

"Your daughter is with her grandmother," I added. "This woman speaks of pain in her hand."

Then, as often happens when I'm bringing messages in, my fingers suddenly appeared to be crippled. Tina looked at my hands and said, "That is how my mom's hands used to get."

"Tina, your mom says thank you for all the prayers."

Tina hugged and kissed me and thanked me profusely.

She claimed communion with her daughter through me made her birthday the best ever.

* * *

I highly recommend that anyone who has lost a loved one join a bereavement group. Each person in the group is going through a range of emotions as he or she copes with loss. Voicing your feelings helps the healing process. Of course, the work I do to ease the grieving process is to bring forth a loved one who has passed over. It is comforting and strengthening to the bereaved person to know that his or her relative or friend is in the safekeeping of God, but even if the group is simply a sharing experience between those left behind, it can be very helpful.

The questions asked by the grieving usually are predictable: "Is my loved one okay?" "Is he angry about the way he left the Earth plane?"

Interestingly, I have never brought forth anyone who is unhappy in the other dimension.

I have heard apologies for events the deceased may have caused while they were on the Earth plane. And I've witnessed repeatedly the peace, love, and everlasting tranquillity that comes to the departed after they've passed on.

I found a profound and moving message printed on a memorial card in a chapel. It is reproduced here. I think it is appropriate to read and reread this lovely poem when you think of your loved ones who have gone on. I regret that I do not know the name of the author:

To Those I Love

When I am gone, release me, let me go. I have so many
things to see and do.

You mustn't tie yourself to me with tears, be happy that
we had so many years.

I gave you my love. You can only guess how much you
gave me in happiness.

But now it's time I traveled on alone.

So grieve awhile for me if grieve you must, then let your
grief be comforted by trust.

It's only for a while that we must part, so bless the
memories within your heart.

I won't be far away, for life goes on. So if you need me,
call and I will come.

Though you can't see or touch me, I'll be near.

And if you listen with your heart you'll hear all of my
love around you soft and clear.

And then when you must come this way alone, I'll greet
you with a smile and say, "Welcome Home."

47. A GIFT BEYOND TIME

*O*ne of the most touching stories I have ever heard was about a beloved mother who departed, leaving behind a gift of love that would be remembered forever by her son and his wife.

This marvelous anecdote came to me from a wonderful lady named Ursula Bacon. It proves how love can survive death and separation and leave an eternal message of affection that time can never erase. I include it here with her permission, in her own words.

"Everybody has heard a few of those uncomplimentary mother-in-law jokes which were popular in the sixties and seventies. Their bad-taste endings rarely left a shred of goodness in the mother-in-law image. In the case of my own mother-in-law, I was lucky. She didn't fit the punch lines.

"My mother-in-law was Mary, and she was a proper lady. The Southern lilt in her voice made even a harsh word sound like a caress, and her off-the-wall feminine logic seemed related to the aphorisms of Gracie Allen of radio and early television fame, whose husband, George Burns, played the straight man.

"Mary was all of five-foot-four, had a youthful figure, a set of legs that would bring tears of envy to a chorus girl's eyes, and a heart the size of Texas. Her generosity was only exceeded by her blindness to the faults of others. God gave us unconditional love—my mother-in-law perfected it.

"During most of her marriage, she had faithfully followed her husband from one US Navy post to the next, setting up house at the drop of a hat, raising two boys and a girl along the way. Her husband was a no-nonsense man of stern behavior and a noticeable lack of self-esteem. He fought his own dark shadows which spilled over into the family life as overly strict military discipline. He ran the house with an iron fist. There was little encouragement for laughter or friendly banter, and social contact with other people was lacking. Mary, on the other hand, was gentle—although feisty when necessary—and eased her husband's harsh ways with love and lighthearted words.

"When the children left home, Mary in a sense left home as well. She worked herself into a prestigious position in a family-held oil company in San Antonio, which gave her the economic freedom to do what she like to do best: bestow gifts, do those extra 'little' things for her children and grandchildren, and come to their rescue when they most needed help. After all, what's a mother for? Mary had a clever way of folding a twenty-dollar bill into a small square and slipping it secretly into a grandchild's hand, a greeting card, or a Christmas stocking. Her generosity to her family knew no boundaries and was limited only by the restrictions of her bank account. And, even then, she managed to perform miracles. There was nothing too small or too big to tackle when it came to 'he'ppin' out the children.

"Mary's husband died when she was sixty-seven, and eight years later she finally retired. It was in the early seventies that I married her oldest son and consequently met Mary. My husband and I were working on a publishing project in Montana when she decided to visit. Mary and I liked each other almost instantly, and at the end of her stay with us and for the rest of her life a deep bond of mutual love and respect kept us in each other's hearts. When she no longer wanted to keep house, she lived with her daughter during the winter and came to us to spend the summers.

"It was during those summers that I really got to know Mary. I watched in amazement as she overlooked everyone's flaws and was able to remove herself from serious problems with no more effort than shooing a pesky fly off a piece of Southern-fried chicken. Typically, she would summarize her philosophy of deal-ing with problems with a smile on her face and a drawl that gave emphasis to her statement, 'Why darlin', nothin's important enough to fuss over and lose sleep. It all comes to pass, it doesn't come to stay.' Who can argue with Southern wisdom?

"She told me stories of her growing up in a little town on the Pamlico Sound in North Carolina where her ancestors had settled. Her descriptions brought to life the unique, independent spirit which belonged solely to that part of America. She personified the kind of grace, charm and down-home humor I refer to as 'those irresistible Southern ways.' I had grown up in Europe and China, and couldn't have presented a life more in contrast to hers. She listened with equal fascination to my tales—two different generations from entirely different backgrounds—two women talking Life.

"The summer Mary visited us in Montana found my husband and me deeply involved in our work and we took little time off for ourselves. Mary knew how much her son liked to go fishing and was forever urging him to 'run along and catch a fish for supper.' Many times she'd push one of her cleverly folded twenties in my hand and insist that I pack a picnic lunch and go off to some wild stream under the Big Sky where the rainbows would be waiting for us.

"Somehow, grateful as we were for her reminders that we should entertain ourselves, we never got away, and before we knew it, it was fall and time for her to return to her winter home in Texas.

"I could not help but notice, almost with surprise, as I assisted Mary with her packing, that the years were catching up with my mother-in-law. She was getting quite frail and fragile. I wanted to hug her to me and whisper, 'Stop the clock, stay young for me, for both of us.'

"We took her to the airport and said our goodbyes.

"As I watched her slight figure walk slowly away from us and disappear into the belly of the big jet, a fleeting moment of bottomless sadness engulfed me. I knew I wasn't going to see her again. She died before the year was out.

"Our work in Montana came to an end and a few days before our return to Oregon we decided to go fishing in the Bitterroot for the last time. I opened the big tackle box we hadn't used for a long time to check if we needed anything. Taped to the inner lid of the tackle box was a white envelope addressed to both of us. It was in Mary's handwriting. My heart missed a beat as I carefully lifted the tape that held the envelope in place, and opened it.

"When I unfolded the white note paper, one of Mary's neatly folded twenty-dollar bills spilled out. Through a veil of tears, I read the note in her fine handwriting:

You must be going fishing if you read this. Have a good time and catch a big one for supper. Love, Mother."

I love Mary's story because it represents a mother's wisdom and understanding of the value of making connections. Of course, it seems obvious in the reading that Mary left her gift to her son and daughter-in-law as a parting gesture, a reminder of the love she felt for the two she was leaving behind. She must have known that her time on Earth was coming to an end, and in the bigness of her heart she wrote the note as a tangible link between the living and the departed—for surely she was deeply aware that her note would not be discovered until after she died.

There is a more profound meaning to Mary's story than its sentimental appeal. It is a reminder of what death teaches us about life. In our culture, death has gradually been removed from family life, in contrast to earlier times when it was regarded as an inevitable presence that drew families closer together and taught them greater appreciation for the joy of living. The rituals that surrounded death helped to teach survivors how to feel about death, and how to relate themselves to the long parade of ancestors who had lived before and to future relatives who would live and die after them. Such a perspective gave family members a greater sense of spiritual security, a strong feeling of position and place in the long drama of generations, and faith that their own ending would be but a new beginning and a reunion with loved ones gone before.

The next chapter explores the idea of learning how to arrive at a more satisfactory relationship with death.

48. LEARNING ABOUT LIFE FROM DEATH

A long time ago, people were more intimate with death and they believed in miracles. Today, even as our population grows older, we are more oriented to preservation of youth than to preparation for dying. Certainly, that cannot be all bad, because it reflects our prolonged vigor, a mental attitude that attainment of sixty or seventy or eighty years of age does not mean the individual should curl up like a shrunken leaf, withdraw from life and wait for death to come.

The fact is, we are living to much older ages than even our most recent forebears. More than half of our national population is over fifty and aging fast.

If there ever was a time in America when we should look to our philosophy about death, it is now. For as we have become more modern, more technologically advanced, it seems as though we have distanced ourselves from the grief ceremonies and memorial observations that we once conducted to see a loved one into the next world. These ceremonies were held to formally say goodbye, and on a deeper level to reestablish our personal identity as a member of a related cluster of humans who had a common ancestral root.

This tradition of death observances and celebrations is largely missing today, depriving us of a crucial and valuable link with those who have gone on.

Think about that. Our link with our parents, uncles, aunts, grandparents, the heroes, villains, explorers and pioneers who populated the past, gives us strong definition, colors our character and plants in us genes of greatness, foolishness, love, mercy and vision. Our progenitors gave us personal history, ideas, courage and inspiration.

Thus, it is sad and makes us less effective as humans to be cut

off from the death process, which makes up the past with its vanished men and women of significance or mediocrity, individuals
from whom we gained our varied inheritances.

Eda LeShan, in her book *Learning to Say Good-by*, captured
our modern dilemma of preferred isolation from death:

> Gradually, death became more removed from daily life.
> Few people died at home. Mostly it was old people who
> died. Children and parents could live for long periods of
> time without ever hearing about the death of someone they
> loved. Unhappily, no generation has ever lived without
> hearing about people dying in wars, and there have been
> terrible wars in the last few generations. But in spite of this,
> the fact of death was seen and talked about less and less. It
> was almost as if people thought that if no one talked about
> death, maybe it would just go away.
>
> During this period, parents were inclined to protect
> their children—they did not take them to funerals, they
> tried not to cry or show their grief in front of their children,
> and they did not talk to them about dying.
>
> Recently, people have begun to realize that such atti-
> tudes were very foolish. When a death occurred, neither
> grownups nor children had any idea what to do or even
> how to feel. And since death had been treated as some-
> thing too ugly and terrible ever to mention, people who
> were dying were often very lonely. Nobody would let them
> talk about their fears; nobody would ever say an honest
> goodbye. And many children grew up feeling very embar-
> rassed about death, not knowing how to act or what to
> say. They wondered about death but were afraid to ask
> any questions.[1]

For various reasons—chiefly the growing impersonality in
our society that distances us from neighbors as well as from our

---

1. Eda LeShan, *Learning to Say Good-by: When a Parent Dies* (New York:
Macmillan, 1976)

own relatives—many of us still do not seem to know what to say about death. We feel embarrassed and uncomfortable about death, and because it's alien to us we shun opportunities to find out about the conclusion in life that, inevitably, each of us will face.

In the previous chapter I told the story of Mary, who left a singular and touching note for her son and daughter-in-law to be found after she died. Now from another friend comes a true story about death that I think illustrates the normal curiosity of children about dying and how its impression on the young can bring home the important lesson playwright George Bernard Shaw taught when he wrote, "Heartbreak is life educating us." In his own words, my friend relates:

"When I was nine years old, I and some other boys who lived in East San Diego used to play baseball on the sandy diamond at our grammar school.

"At the end of the diamond, across an alleyway, there were several buildings whose rear entrances faced the school yard. There was a drugstore, a five-and-dime, a small grocery, a hardware store, and on the corner was a funeral home.

"I can't remember which of the boys on our baseball team told us that a pretty teenage girl had died and was lying in her casket in the viewing room of the funeral home.

"Immediately all of us were fascinated and curious about the dead girl. Not one of us had ever attended a funeral. I, for one, had never seen a dead person. In those days, television was still a miracle that was just starting up and there were no pictures of dead or dying people to educate us. Another decade would pass before the new visual journalism would present us with images of living and dying that startled and horrified us.

"As children sometimes do, the group of us standing on the baseball diamond that late, sunny afternoon made an unusual decision. We agreed to knock at the front door of the funeral home and politely ask for permission to view the dead girl.

"There were six of us from our team, laden with baseball gloves, two wooden bats and a catcher's mask, who waited at the impressive black-painted front door of the funeral home with its discreet bright brass nameplate above the shiny door handle. We could hear the chimes of the doorbell ring distantly in the interior, announcing our presence, and soon approaching footsteps. Facing us when the door swung open was a tall man with bushy eyebrows and a stern face. He was dressed in a sharply pressed dark suit. He looked at us in surprise, then said, 'What can I do for you, boys?'

"I had been selected as spokesman, and said with a dry mouth, 'Sir, we found out that a girl has died and you have her here. We don't know her name, but we wondered, well, if we could see her.'

"The solemn expression on the man's face seemed to melt away as he examined each of us with his probing eyes. His dark gaze seemed to strip away our courage and laid bare our innocence. Like the others, I wished I were anyplace but where I was standing.

"In a soft voice, he said, 'None of you has ever seen a dead person, is that right?'

" 'Yes, sir,' we all mumbled. I think every one of us at that moment felt foolish, a little frightened at the impulse that had taken us on such a strange errand. I know that I felt a prickle of shame to have presented myself to the immaculate stranger in a dusty sweatshirt, scuffed tennis shoes and faded jeans. I desperately wanted to escape.

"But suddenly, with a warm smile, the man swung the door open wider. 'Come on in, boys,' he said. 'Leave your baseball gear in the hallway.'

"Astonished and subdued, all of us entered the funeral home, deposited our gloves, balls and bats on a wooden bench in the hallway, and followed our escort across the soundless carpet into a softly lighted room. In one corner, surrounded by a faint pink glow of indirect lighting, was a white casket, lined with rose satin that fell into smooth, straight folds to the carpeted floor.

"Our tall guardian of the dead beckoned to me with his finger and I was the first to look upon the face and form of a lovely girl, about sixteen, who lay as though asleep on her cushion of satin. Her thick, brown hair, arranged around her oval face in a half halo, framed her features with a soft focus. Her loveliness took my breath away. Her lips were lightly painted with lipstick and her closed eyes were shaded delicately with a faint blue overtone. Her skin was lightly powdered and cheekbones were colored with a rose blush. She appeared to be asleep, but there was a final stillness about her form that convinced me that I would never see her modest breasts rise and fall with inspiration. She was dressed in a plain, white silk gown, with a row of covered buttons ranging from the soft, rounded collar that circled her neck and descended to her waist. Her hands and arms were folded against her chest, crossing at the wrists, in the typical arrangement that indicated final rest, although I did not know that at the time.

"I stared at the girl for perhaps two or three minutes, long enough to sense the impatience of the boys standing behind me, waiting for their turn to look at death in a lovely form.

"After awkwardly whispering 'Thank you' to the kindly funeral director who had been standing quietly near the head of the casket, I walked slowly in the hallway where we had left our baseball gear. I tried to understand my confused feelings, but my one overwhelming emotion was immense awe mixed with regret. And beneath that, as though the ache in my heart was like a deep well filled with sorrow and loss, was an engulfing sadness. I remember also that as I stood alone waiting in the hallway for the others, a hymn from my mother's church popped into my head. It was 'The Old Rugged Cross,' and from that moment on, whenever I heard that sad refrain I associated it with the dead girl and the lump that formed in my throat. My eyes were moist with unshed tears and I fought to keep them inside me, because it wasn't manly to cry and show weakness to the others.

"We all dispersed quickly and set out for home on our separate paths, with no conversation, except, 'See ya later.' I assumed correctly that each of my teammates was overwhelmed. They, no more than I, could talk about the lovely girl who should have grown to maturity, married, had children and died when she was an old lady. For many years after visiting the girl in her casket, I dreamed and wondered about her, caught in an eternal sleep from which she would never open her eyes.

"I never told anybody in my family about our visit to the funeral home. I did not wish to share my private thoughts, because I had not come to a conclusion about my own attitude toward death. I thought about dying from time to time in the years after I saw the girl, but because my immediate family was intact, death wasn't a morbid happening that threatened me, my parents, or my brother and sister.

"When my grandfather died in North Carolina, probably a year or so after my visit to the funeral home, and my mother flew east to his wake, I was very little affected because we children did not know him well. I remembered him mistily as a tall, affable man who smoked a pipe and had the aroma of Prince Albert tobacco in his clothes, and who poured his breakfast coffee into a saucer so that he could blow it cool with his breath.

"I eventually learned that death is an event for which we must prepare, and that meant developing a personal philosophy of life, one which took me many years to formulate."

As my friend indicated, formulating a philosophy about life and death is important for the reasons I listed early in this chapter. I also think it is worthwhile to consider what you may do to keep the memory of a loved one alive so that the continuity of your immediate and extended family can be preserved for future children.

After a lifetime of thinking about death, listening to voices from the other side, counseling grieving survivors to accept their loss and move forward, and witnessing spirits who have made appearances after the death of their bodies, I have come up with four suggestions that readers may wish to apply to their lives when they are facing the death of a loved one.

These suggestions also form the basis of information parents can call upon to educate their children about dying.

1. *Start a chart of your family's personal history.* If you capture your parents' and grandparents' memories and recollections of

their lives, you will have created a "living" biography from which your family history can be constructed.

This is not a new idea, but it becomes more important today because the old-fashioned family has deteriorated. We are not as close to cousins, aunts and uncles, even parents and grandparents as we used to be. That is unfortunate, for as a result of our isolation and separateness we have lost contact with our family heritage.

It is comforting, satisfying and stabilizing to have a sense of who, not just where, we came from. To know that Great-great-uncle Joe was a blackbirder, a slave trader who profited from human cargoes sold at auction, may be disturbing, but his dark deeds may be balanced on the scales of your family history by courageous men and women who saved lives in the Civil War.

Your past is rich in human anecdotes, in love, hate and forgiveness—part of the vigorous human stream. Not to know them all, the heroes and villains, and the parts your parents and grandparents played in the long drama is to make folly of death and to forever lose vital links in the human trail that contributed to who you are.

Never forget that your mother and father, and their parents before them, were different from anyone else in the world. They were one of a kind, just as you are, an individual who is his own unique design. It is because of that uniqueness that the heartbreak of having a parent, or a child, or a grandparent die is so devastating. Such deaths teach us how valuable a human can be. Because each one of us is special, one of a kind, one who can never come again in the same pattern, we feel the death of one as terribly painful. Other people may find our love, but each love is a star that shines with a very special light in our heart.

It can be a real effort to get parents and grandparents to dig into the past to reveal who they have been and to describe their own parents and grandparents. But there are no other sources from which you gain valuable information if they pass on and leave an empty silence behind.

I've discovered that using a tape recorder is an easy method to get parents and grandparents to talk and reminisce, to remember events and actions that come to the surface with a little prodding from you.

2. *Teach your children what you have learned about death.* Make them understand that it is as much a part of life as breathing. If you believe in an afterlife, explain your views to them. You may wish to use the Holy Bible, the Koran or the Torah as a reference point, depending on your religious persuasion.

Do not allow your children to form a viewpoint about death from television. Almost unfailingly, television provides false and misleading ideas about death by promoting programs of violence and callousness in depictions of death. Children may adopt such ideas, and if uncorrected, these become a twisted interpretation of how to view life and death.

3. *For the more adventuresome—consult a genuine clairvoyant who can introduce you to the world beyond the grave.* Always ask for references and check the reputation of any psychic you may use.

In the same general category of the spiritual are respected masters who teach meditation, centering, and a variety of methods which reveal how to go inside to contact the "genius within," the God of the universe who is present in each of us. Such revelations, as you may discover, will certainly alter your previous ideas about dying.

4. *Learn how to grieve and teach your children by example.* There are several good books on grieving. One I strongly recommend is *Death: The Final Stage of Growth,* by Elisabeth Kübler-Ross.

My bereavement work has brought me in contact with many people who have lost children, parents, brothers and sisters. Sometimes the person is newly bereaved, and sometimes he may have lost a loved one many years earlier. In either case, the person is suffering a deep wound of loss that does not seem to heal. I find it a heartwarming experience to witness the expression of such a person when he or she realizes that the messages I bring from across the chasm actually come from the loved one he or she is pining for.

My methods, of course, are a very nontraditional mode of grief counseling. But I have discovered that if the survivors are convinced their missing ones are happy in their new lives, their grief abates, replaced with awe and wonder.

A common emotion in many bereavement sessions is guilt. Did we do enough for the absent loved one in her final days?

I deeply believe that through the agonizing process of grief, each prayer offered is a way of helping a loved one who has passed over and helping ourselves adjust. Many times I have heard those on the other side admonish a family member to move forward, to remember happy times and forget the anguish or pain the deceased went through just before his passing.

It is terribly difficult to watch someone we love leave the Earth plane, or to know that this person is going to be leaving shortly. I have learned that it helps dying people on their voyage for us to express love and appreciation for them, and to assure them that their final decision to leave is one that we must not hinder by our own deep sense of impending loss.

Our tears release our anxiety and anger, and help us cope with the impending loss. Just as the ocean was created with salt and can heal our wounds, so can the salt of our tears help us recover from grief.

I believe that when we enter the Earth plane, just before our first breath, we are given the secrets of life and the choice to accept or reject them. As we take our first breath, we begin the process of death: it is always just a breath away.

49. PSYCHICS AND READING TOOLS

*M*any people have asked me to determine whether a psychic is genuine. While many people claim to be "psychic," usually they are only highly intuitive or experience occasional ESP. The following information will help readers to make intelligent choices as to the genuineness of the psychic they propose to use.

People with psychic abilities usually acquire their talent in one of two ways: they are either born with them or the gifts appear when they are faced with life-threatening traumas. If a person is born with psychic ability, he begins to manifest his talents in early childhood.

Responsible psychics do not encourage their clients to return for regular or frequent readings, because they don't want them to depend on the readings to make decisions. Instead, readings should be used as one of many tools to facilitate growth.

Methods of readings vary with the psychic's preferred style. There are many different types of tools that can be used during a reading. Psychics may use a combination of tarot cards, crystal balls, palmistry, tea leaves or photographs.

I should make an important point here: there are many psychics who, unfortunately, are cynical and dishonest about the revelations they make. In my own case, I made an investigation of how other readers handled themselves and how they delivered their messages. I visited about twenty psychic readers in the New York area. According to my estimate, only ten percent were totally accurate. However, I was not merely assessing their accuracy rate; I was examining their techniques and their honesty. I learned that each psychic must develop his own way of expressing candor and love, and, most of all, must understand his or her clients' fears. Today, it is so easy to pick up the phone and dial a psychic. In fact, to work as a telephone psychic, all you need is a deck of tarot cards. I am not implying that all phone psychics are incapable of valuable insights. There are some truly gifted psychics working the phones, but there are others whose sense of responsibility to a bereaved person seeking solace is highly questionable.

If a so-called psychic claims that you have barriers in your life such as money or relationship problems, or difficulties with work, and she can remove them by using a ritual or prayer for a large sum of money, I suggest that you refuse. Such a person is taking advantage of you. Give your trust and faith to God and place your difficulties in his hands. Any person claiming to be very clairvoyant and putting a high price on his or her disclosures should be avoided.

One example of fraud came to my attention when a young woman phoned me. I had given her a reading two weeks before her call. She explained she needed to see me immediately because another reader insisted that she could bring the woman's ex-boyfriend back for $5,000. I told her it was not necessary for her to see me and certainly not to give the reader one red cent. I hope she took my advice.

I think it is a wonderful experience to have a consultation with a psychic. However, you must always remember to be discerning and discard any information or advice that you do not think is appropriate. If a psychic somehow frightens you, do not carry the burden of her words. Everything you are told does not mean that it will come to full fruition.

I received a phone call from another young woman, named Jennifer, who told me that she had just left a reader's home. This reader had told her that her mother was going to die within the next few weeks. Jennifer was so frantic that I arranged an appointment with her immediately.

When Jennifer arrived she was still shaken from the psychic's words. I told Jennifer that it was not her mother's time, and that she would not be dying within the next few weeks. Jennifer asked me if I was certain of this, and I assured her that I was positive the other reader was wrong and her mother was not failing in any way. As Jennifer and I continued talking, she calmed down. This happened some time ago and Jennifer's mother is still with us.

When you make arrangements for a reader, you should be aware that an honest psychic will establish the fee before the reading and ask for nothing beyond this. At one time I could not understand why there had to be an exchange of money for the messages that came to me so easily. Now, I understand that one of the primary reasons for exchanging money is so that the client and I build no collective karma with each other. The exchange of money is similar to the exchange of energy. Paying a fee also gives the client an incentive to appreciate and to listen closely to the messages that are delivered.

50. YOUR DIVINE DESTINY

I have read much about death and the mystery of the soul. The words of one spiritual master, Sai Baba, who lives in India, have been very helpful in opening my mind and heart. He offers wisdom about our true nature as spiritual beings who never die. Like the commandment given by Jesus in the New Testament to "love one another," Baba's writings are a message of love, stating again and again that all is possible through love. "Love can transform man into a divine being, it helps him to manifest the divine, which is his core," writes Baba. Such beautiful messages are full of truth, and reading books by spiritual masters like Sai Baba do not take anything away from my faith or practice as a Catholic. On the contrary, they help me find even more meaning in the words of Jesus, and strengthen my Christian faith. It is my belief that all religions point to God, and we are each blessed to find a path that leads us to Him.

Sai Baba writes, "There is only one royal road for the spiritual journey—love. Love all beings as manifestations of the same divinity that is the very core of yourself. Love all beings, that is enough." Jesus' first commandment was just as simple and direct. He taught us that the most important thing in life is to love one another, and to treat everyone we meet as if they were God himself.

I believe my experience with visitors from the "other side" has led me to understand that the only way to God is through self-knowing, dying to outer self, and being born to a deeper inner self—the silent place where God lives inside each of us.

Jesus taught that the best way to commune with God is to enter that silent place, rather than to stand up in public and just mouth the words of prayers. "When you pray, go to your private room, shut yourself in, and so pray to your Father who is in that secret place, and your Father who sees all that is done in secret will reward you" (Matthew 6:6). I believe that the "private room" Jesus describes is our inner self, the place we enter when we close our eyes and forget everything but God. Without this silence, it's difficult to hear the soft, subtle messages that are waiting to be heard.

Imagine sitting in a room with a radio blaring full blast beside you, and someone speaking softly to you from the other side of the room. You can't hear a word the person is saying. But once you turn off the radio, you can hear the person perfectly. For me, this is how prayer works. When I take a few minutes to slow down, turn off my thoughts and my worries, I clear the way so that God's voice can be heard. I believe God is always speaking to us, but we just don't turn down the noise in our minds to a level where we can hear that quiet voice.

Everyone has the ability to get close to God through prayer or, as some call it, meditation. I believe that everyone also shares the ability, to some degree, to pick up messages from loved ones who have passed over, if we would only pay attention. I'm certain that many people have been given tiny clues that are messages of comfort that a loved one is alive and well in the spiritual realm. But like me, when I first saw my father's flag lying mysteriously on my sister's floor, we can be fearful of these messages, or just ignore them. In my life, I have found that the universe is always sending me messages.

For example, when my sister Connie went into the hospital for surgery, I was hopeful that everything would go well, but naturally I was concerned. Three small events that day took my worries away. I interpreted each of these events as a little sign from the universe, telling me that things would be fine.

The first event was a greeting from the parking lot attendant, whom I recognized from my last visit to the hospital thirteen years earlier when my mother was hospitalized there. He was very friendly, and we chatted about how long it had been since we'd seen each other. He told me that he'd been working there for fourteen years. I immediately connected that number to the Archangel Michael, whose spiritual number is fourteen. Archangel Michael is a strong protector, and I felt that this message was a nod from him.

The second message came later, in the hospital cafeteria. I was having coffee, and the friend who accompanied me that day ordered tea. There were many teas to choose from, but she ordered one that smelled like strawberries. This scent made me think of the strawberry malteds my mother always requested in the hospital. The strawberry smell came with a comforting feeling, and I knew things would be okay with Connie.

The third event happened in the family waiting area outside surgery. Suddenly, the doctor who had worked with my mother thirteen years earlier walked by. He had not seen me in all those years, but stopped to say hello. He said he rarely went to that part of the hospital, so it was a real chance reunion for us. But I knew better. This was the third message of reassurance from the universe I would receive that day.

By the time Connie was wheeled into the recovery room, I had no doubts that she was fine. Her surgery did, in fact, go perfectly.

When we open our eyes and our hearts, I believe we can receive many little messages like this every day. You don't have to be a psychic or a spiritual master to hear the voice of God, who speaks through ordinary things and inside us, in our secret room. We are all capable of extraordinary things, because we've been created in the image of God. In the words of Sai Baba, our potential is very, very high:

> Man is not just a creature with hands and feet and eyes and ears and head and trunk. He is much more than the total of all these organs and parts. They are but the crude image that came out of the mold. Later, they have to be ground and scraped, polished, perfected, smoothened, softened, through the intellect and higher impulses. Then man becomes the ideal candidate for divinity which is his real destiny.[1]

1. Samuel H. Sandweiss, M.D., *Spirit and the Mind* (San Diego, CA: Birth Day Publishing Company, 1985), p. 184.

As part of learning to say goodbye to loved ones and accepting that their destiny and yours when the time comes is a new life, I have presented stories of my personal encounters with men and women who desperately wish to be able to believe that their loved ones who have passed over are safe and happy in a brighter dimension. All of us crave proof of life hereafter. Yet the proof is all around us, the evidence of which comes to us in the form of miracles, answers to prayers, and testimony and recitations of messages from those beyond.

The problem for the survivor who has lost a loved one is of what and whom to believe. Whose interpretation of death should he or she, suffering the pain of loss, believe? It is easy for the pragmatists to say life ends at the grave, because there is no substantive evidence that it goes on. It takes far more courage, and more personal inspiration, to stretch the soul to embrace an unseen future that promises a reunion of the spirit with its origin-maker-God.

From the depth of my heart, I hope that my story of spiritual awakening, and of my experiences with those who have made contact with departed loved ones, have given you a new awareness of your constant contact with God and your loved ones, your immortality and your divine destiny.

ABOUT THE AUTHOR

Reverend Edward N. Tabbitas, known to his friends and clients as "Reverend Ed," has been able to communicate with the spiritual realm since the age of seven. In his work as a spiritual counselor and healer, he uses his gifts to reach into the dimensions of the spirit world to bring forth loved ones who have passed over. His dedication comes from his love of fellow humans and his desire to help ease their pain and anguish during the loss of a loved one. Reverend Ed's mission is to act as a communication relay between the boundaries of life and death, and also to bring a sense of comfort and understanding to the bereaved by peeking beyond the veil on their behalf.

If you would like to write to Reverend Ed to share a spiritual experience or inquire about scheduling a session, please send correspondence to: Edward Nunzio Tabbitas, 14 Belfield Avenue, Staten Island, NY 10312.

The Common Heart
An Experience of Interreligious Dialogue
NETANEL MILES-YEPEZ

For twenty years, a group of spiritual seekers from many religious traditions met in various places around the United States under the rubric of the Snowmass Conferences to engage in the deepest form of interreligious dialogue. Participants include Fr. Thomas Keating, Roshi Bernie Glassman, Swami Atmarupananda, Dr. Ibrahim Gamard, Imam Bilal Hyde, Pema Chödrön, Rabbi Henoch Dov Hoffman, and many others.

The Uttermost Deep
The Challenge of Painful Near-Death Experiences
GRACIA FAY ELLWOOD

"An extremely valuable and seminal contribution to our understanding of NDEs [Near Death Experiences]."—**Kenneth Ring**, PhD, Professor Emeritus of Psychology, University of Connecticut, author of *Heading Toward Omega* and *Lessons from the Light*.

she had probably saved. But the thought didn't do much to make her feel better. Maybe if he was moving it would. Kat got another cup of cold water and dumped it on his face. He stirred a bit. Waiting for him to wake up, Kat gathered the evidence of her being there. She pocketed the postcard, reached under the dresser for the pepper spray, looked for Kyle's car keys and found them in his pants, then finally she picked up the camera. It was hers now. Had to be.

She moved the pillow from his face. The low moan started again.

"Kyle...fucko...can you hear me?" His lower lip quivered trying to answer. Giving up, he nodded. His puffy eyes were still shut but fluttering.

"Good...now listen, this whole event is on tape, I'm taking it with me. If you ever try to find me or harm me again I will post the damn video on the web for everyone to see. You think a punch on stage was embarrassing? Just wait until you see this. And don't think you're going to get it back. I'm going to put it in a safety deposit box and leave explicit instructions that if anything happens to me to have it posted. GOT IT?"

Tears started to pour out of his wounded eyes. She couldn't tell if they were from pain, guilt or fear. Maybe all three. He nodded. Kat was amazed that all had come out of her mouth. She hadn't even thought about it before hand. The last thing she did was un-cuff one hand, leaving him locked to the bed, and then she put the phone next to him. Knowing he couldn't see and with the pain he was in she hoped it would take him a few hours to call for help.

Kat got to the door and looked back. She'd done it. *We did it*, she thought. Jasper and she. Opening the door she was accosted by the brightest sun and hottest blast of air she'd ever felt. Her eyes stung from the light (not nearly as much as Kyle's eyes stung) but she welcomed it. She had thought she was never going to see the sun again.

7

Kat drove the speed limit back to her car, fearful of getting pulled over in a stolen car. Again, the road was deserted when she arrived at her car. Shaking, she popped open the trunk to get rid of the pot. Throwing it in his car would top things off. When the lid bounced to it's fully open position Kat suspected to see a big block wrapped in saran wrap like in the movies. But all she saw was her suitcases. Thinking he would hide it so it wouldn't look suspicious she dug through them. Nothing. She looked through every inch of the trunk and found no signs of any drug. Rubbed it in the fibers her ass. Then something familiar caught her eye. A tiny flash of pink.

Kat unzipped the tiny pouch of her largest suitcase. She hadn't bothered to check it since it was too small for anything put paper, and that's where she found it. One small pink sticky note that read: *"Gotcha! Thanks for the lay!"* First, she was pissed for being so easily duped. How stupid could she have been? But then again it had worked out for her, for lots of women. She crumpled it up and tossed it on the hood of his car.

"No...got you Kyle!"

Having never done it before, it took her nearly an hour to change the flat. It would hold for now, she thought as she got in the car and put the top down. As Kat drove down the street she watched Kyle's car get smaller and smaller just like she had watched hers just a few hours ago. She was relieved and invigorated. Kat was definitely not the same woman who had left Massachusetts a few months ago.

This morning, Kat had left the nasty hotel not knowing where to spread Jasper's ashes or what state to go to next. Little did she know the ashes would be spread in a sleazy sex motel. After the day's events she knew where she was headed. She most definitely knew.

Kyle woke up in the hospital one day after missing his show for the first time in his career. He opened his eyes and saw nothing but flashes of pain. They were covered with gauze. He only knew he was in a hospital because he felt a remote next to his stomach. When he pushed its buttons the bed moved up. He wasn't sure if he had called for help or if a maid had found him. The day's events were blurry. After what seemed like an eternity without answers to questions about the extent of his damage was, a nurse (or so he assumed since it was a woman) came to tell him.

His eyes had severe damage to the corneas. They should heal within a few months, but only time would tell if his vision would ever be a hundred percent. As for his groin, that's where the bad news came in. His penis and testicles were so badly damaged that they'd had to be removed to enable him to urinate properly. He had a catheter in now. She went on to explain that he was going to have to undergo dozens of skin grafts over the course of the next few months. She kept going on and on about medical procedures, how they had to take skin from his back for the grafts, hearing this he had tuned her out. No penis…that's all that ran through his head. He refused to believe it. It felt like it was still there. He wanted to grab it to make sure, but his hands were tied down. The nurse said something about keeping him from damaging it in his sleep. He started to panic. The blipping noise next to his head sped up until the nurse pricked him with something. Sleep followed.

The next time he woke up (which could have been five minutes or three years, he couldn't tell) he heard two male voices. They said they were cops. Kyle flat out refused to talk to them. When he wouldn't speak the one with the gravelly voice barked.

"Look you pervert, I don't care what kind of sick stuff you like to do in the bedroom. All we want to know is do you want to press charges on someone, were you attacked, or what?"

Kyle told them to fuck off. He presumed they did since he didn't hear anything else said. The rest of his waking time was spent thinking of one thing, Kat. He wasn't so much pissed at her, as he was amazed that she had tricked and defeated him. It made him want her more. He felt himself getting an erection. A penis-less erection, since his member was in a biohazard bin in the basement of the hospital.

It wasn't until three weeks later when the eye gauze came off that he saw it was actually gone. He had been told many times but had refused to believe it until he saw it with his own eyes. He had tried to touch the region dozens of times over the past few weeks but it was just too damn sore. His heart sank. The desire for Kat turned to rage. His passion for life (which was miniscule to begin with) faded. The thought of never being able to cum again was too much.

One month to the day after being released from the hospital, a partially blind and castrated Kyle Winterbourne did one last magic trick. He disappeared. Though he had few coworkers and fewer friends, rumors about him surfaced for months in the magic industry. Some said he was in seclusion deep in the mountains, preparing for a huge comeback. Few joked that he died testing out a new trick. But most said he just plain old killed himself. Only Kyle will ever know the truth behind his final trick.

8

Not having Kat around ended up being the best thing for Val. She spent every second with Trevor (or as Kat had called him-Val's mystery man). They rode horses, went hiking, swimming and ate every meal together that weekend. Kat had practically left her mind for the first time in ages. For some strange reason she wasn't worried about her - she was going to be just fine.

The only time she really gave Kat much thought was when she saw Billy walking with his head down (which was every time they saw him that weekend). He would look at her like a puppy asking for a bone, and then ask if she had heard anything. She got so sick of it that she gave Kat's cell number to him.

Billy felt like a hole the size of Texas was in his heart. Guilt weighed down his feet making them drag behind as walked. Buck even taught the riding lessons for him that weekend so he could…well mope around some more. After getting her cell phone number he must have called it a few hundred times. But not once did he leave a message. What could he say? Sorry? But he wasn't. It was the single best kiss of his life. Yes he was sorry she ran but he knew it was because she had felt it too: that swelling in the heart, the release of adrenaline, the natural high that felt so good you just wanted it again and again.

Billy thought about trying to track her down and profess his love to her and try to talk her into not being scared. To tell her he'd wait as long as he had to. But he chose to tell himself that the chances of finding her were minuscule (even thought the real reason was he couldn't stand the thought of getting his heart broken). He was happy that his old drinking buddy Trevor Wilson and Val had hooked up. That gave him a tremendous leg up in the whole Kat situation. If Val fell in love with him she would visit the ranch. If Val kept visiting, maybe Kat would come with her. It was a long shot but it was all he had to keeping him going.

Most of all Billy couldn't wait for Monday, the day he got to go see Johnny. If he found out what was wrong with him and helped, maybe Kat would come back to thank him. Again, he was grabbing at stars, but he needed something. There was no way he was going to give up.

Reluctantly Val left on Monday, as planned. The good-bye was long and sad. She felt so close to Trevor, especially after they'd made love this morning. That night they had decided to hold off until they saw each other again. When they awoke not a word was spoken. It just happened, it felt natural and right.

Val couldn't believe she came here thinking she was going to have to pull Kat out of falling in love and instead she fell in love herself. She tried not to get up too much hope. He did live a few thousand miles away after all. But she couldn't help it. On her layover in St. Louis she called him. They talked for the entire hour like a couple that had been going out for years. *Finally*, Val thought…finally.

Monday morning Kat found herself leaving Iowa. Though she was traveling the straightest line she could, Kat couldn't help but dip in to Illinois (while leaving Missouri) to knock off another state on the way to Minnesota. While driving the long stretches of desolate road, Kat tallied the number of states in her head. Twenty-five. Half way there.

How the hell did she think she'd be done now? There was a lot of backtracking to do. That would add a tremendous amount of more time. But then again, what was the rush? Still, Kat felt like there was a reason she wanted to hurry, she felt like there was something at the end waiting for her.

The past day and a half Kat had felt like she was driving forever even though earlier in the trip she had driven many more hours in a row. Maybe it was the flat openness that made the roads feel like they had no end. On one particular stretch Kat thought maybe she did die back in the jungle room and she was now stuck in Hell. An eternity of driving in a straight line. The road was so long, and empty, with nothing for the eyes to feast on but fields of crops. She yearned for a gas station, diner, park, store… anything, damn it, to get her eyes off the streaks of green and brown.

At one point Kat got so delirious that she stopped the car and did a Chinese fire drill. She screamed at the top of her lungs and ran around the car several times. No one passed, of course. She wished someone would have driven by, pointed and laughed. At least then she would know it wasn't Hell. Back in the car she was so bored with music that she decided to check her messages. She hadn't since leaving the ranch. She bet there was probably a dozen.

Punching in her code she smiled to herself anticipating the heartfelt worried messages. She felt a bit hurt when there was only one. It was Val, sounding almost like she was forced to leave it. It was brief, stating for her to call and let them know she was all right. She tossed the phone back in the purse, disappointed. It was another twelve miles before she knew it wasn't Hell. A brightly glowing McDonalds pleased her eyes. It was a much-welcomed sight.

Neither hungry nor needing to pee, Kat pulled in to ease her mind. Inside was the usual crowd of kids eating nuggets and fries with one stressed parent munching on a Big Mac only to regret not getting a salad when they weighed themselves later that week. Then there was the group of elderly men that seemed to always take over a corner or two to complain about pretty much everything. Being inside the restaurant Kat felt like she was right back in her hometown. It was even the same design and had pretty much the same décor. Even the pimply kids behind the counter goofed off and ignored customers just like at home.

Kat ordered a ten-piece nugget and asked for extra sweet and sour sauce before taking a neutral seat in-between the group of people just starting their lives and the group just ending theirs. It felt like home. It was a warm feeling, a good feeling. She missed home but knew deep down she would never go back there. Really, what was the point? A little kid to her left stole some fries from his sister. They bickered, and the exhausted mom who snipped at them looked like she needed a six-month vacation as she told them to cut it out or else Dad would get angry. Kat would give anything to be that woman. She might look miserable but she was lucky.

Kat looked the other way. Six old men sat around, only one had food, the rest had coffee that they didn't sip. One man complained about the President doing one thing or the other but before he could finish three others jumped on his words to cut him off. She wondered how many countless hours they spent here, fighting about the same things over and over again. Another man (the fattest of the group) started complaining about his wife who thought the President was cute. They all yelled at that one. Then the wife hating began. Kat would give anything to have her wrinkly husband complain about her.

Though it felt like home, the more she listened to everyone the more she felt like an outsider. Not because of the location but because she was alone. But this time the emptiness was different. It wasn't from missing Jasper, it was just missing having someone to talk to. The last week at the ranch had been wonderful. She only wished she could go back, but it was too late for that now. Besides, she had a promise to keep.

Thinking about the promise she realized this could be a celebratory meal. She should be happy not depressed. She was half done. Twenty-five states was a dang lot. This was the halfway point! And twenty-six was just a few hours away. Forcing herself, Kat cheered up a bit and bought two apple pies. She never much liked microwave pies but today she had a taste for them. Outside she sat on a bench by the play zone. Amazingly the bench was hotter than the apple pies. It was a scorcher. So hot, in fact, that all the kids were inside leaving the play area empty.

Swallowing the last glob of apple cinnamon goo from the small cardboard box, Kat thought of her plan for Minnesota. How do you approach the man who killed your husband?

9

Last night while sitting in a forgettable hotel eating an even more forgettable dinner, Kat started to make some phone calls. Getting the killer's address was a lot harder than she had thought it would be. She called the police station back home and asked to talk to the detective who had handled her husband's death (not realizing it was a Sunday night). Almost no one was there. The worst part was that she could barely remember the name (which was odd since the fact that he lived in Minnesota was burned in her mind). But with a few fake tears she got the officer on duty to pull the file. Kat had no clue whether or not he was breaking the law but with the amount of huffs and puffs the man performed she thought it might be a felony.

She wrote down the name, Don McAlister, but he refused to give out the address even when she balled louder. After a few sweet pleases, she gave up on him. A name and a state wasn't much, especially when it was a state as big as Minnesota. Then she remembered Buck from D.C. (saying his name to herself she realized that she had never known a Buck until a month ago and now she knew two. Odd.) It took a lot of digging through her bags and several trips to the car to find his number. She cursed herself for not putting it in her cell. Finally at eight-thirty, she gave him a ring.

He answered with a *who the hell is calling me on a Sunday night* tone. It took him a few silent seconds to remember her. Then, with concern in her voice, he asked how she was holding up…Kat actually wanted to tell him all about Kyle. She found herself not able to blurt it out fast enough. The man chuckled a pleasant sounding laugh every time Kat sounded excited. She wondered if telling an ex-government employee about committing a crime was a smart thing, but when Buck bellowed a big *"Good job! You did the world a great service, woman!"* Kat felt her cheeks blush.

After the story, Kat sensed he was ready to hang up thinking she had called to just tell him the good news (well good for her and many women but bad for the mutilated magician). So she quickly blurted out,

"But that's not what I called for…" She could hear him sigh. His mind must be racing with what it could be. At the same moment she heard a woman yell something in the background. The phone went scratchy for a second, mumbling, scratchy, then he was back with a *sorry.*

"Look I know this is wrong of me to ask a favor but I didn't know who else to call. Is there any way you could find out the address of someone for me?" Kat heard what sounded like his teeth being sucked. She couldn't tell if it was a good thing or bad.

"Well of course I can, Mrs. Cutter. But first you must explain and validate it. I could get in a lot of trouble if no good came of it."

The truth was Kat didn't know what she would do at the sight of the man. Flip out and attack? Cry? Run? Whatever it was she needed to lie right now and hope later on it wouldn't be a lie.

Once again Kat was amazed at how she could weave a web of lies. She definitely wasn't the person she always thought she was. He did feel bad for her and only agreed after she put out some more of those fake tears. An hour later he called back with the information. 361 Raymond Drive, Calmare, Minnesota.

She promised to be good, hung up and went searching the map for it. She couldn't find it though. She wanted to call him back and double-check but that would have been pushing it. Finally around nine she asked the front desk if they had an Internet café in town. They didn't, but for five dollars an hour they would let her use the computer in the office. Kat paid ten and stayed every second of the two hours in front of the screen.

At first she was a bit hesitant to research the man - nervous what she might find. So instead, she checked her email. The Yahoo account had a warning message on it for being full. Two hundred and something emails awaited her. Kat glanced over them, most were junk, others were from the few so-called friends back home. She was ready to hit the delete all button when she saw the bottom few were from CowBill@BBRanch.com.

Her finger floated above the delete button. She didn't know if she wanted to read them or not. Of course she did. Desperately. But the fear of wanting him was starting to overtake her. She clicked on the four emails from him then deleted all the rest in her box. The box shrank from nine pages to a half. Only four emails were left highlighted reading *New*. All four were titled *Please Read, Please*.

Kat sat looking at the screen, wanting to read them. After a while the screen changed over to fish swimming around a tank. She knew she was wasting too much time. Not knowing when the next time she might get to use a computer would be, she printed off each one doing her best not to read anything on them. The printer was quiet and she was glad, the front desk didn't say anything about using it. From what Kat could tell, two of the emails were about a paragraph or two long. The other two were a few pages. The printer kicked off and its cooling fan slowed to a hum. Kat grabbed the papers and folded them into four. She tucked them into the seat of her pants and changed the screen to Yahoo search.

All she could find was driving directions to Calmare and a sight or two about how it was a ghost town. *How appropriate,* she thought. One of the pages went on to say it was an old mining town. Kat couldn't figure out what the Hell it was mining and didn't care. The site went on to say it only had three hundred people living there. That made the place all the creepier to Kat. She told herself that the computer must be wrong, it had to have its Wal-Marts and McDonalds.

Yet, the more she searched the more she found on how it was practically an abandoned town. Printing off the directions, once again nervous of getting caught Kat went on to search for Don McAlister. A little over three thousand matches came up. Yet, none matched what she was actually looking for. Oh well she'd just have to go into this blindly with an address and a name.

After checking her mail and doing the searches she had twenty minutes left. She spent it just surfing around looking up good celebrity gossip and movie reviews. She hadn't seen a movie since the Mel Gibson one that brought back her sex drive. Thinking of it brought the tingling feeling to her area. She was about to leave early and go back to her room for a date with herself when flashes of Kyle half naked and hard came into her mind. The tingling quickly went away.

Kat knew it had been too good. No nightmares, hardly any regret and the images had practically left her mind. The vivid picture of his melting skin and the look on his face afterwards ruined the sensation below. She knew something like this was going to happen sooner or later. She actually feared a breakdown of guilt. Having the images flash in her mind actually made her happy. Not the mental pictures of them but because she knew guilt was still a part of her.

Going to meet the man who had killed her husband was a lot of pressure. She was scared she might kill him. Though it was a long shot she was still scared she might do something drastic since she hadn't felt guilt over what she had done to Kyle. And he only tried to rape her, not kill someone she loved. The last ten minutes or so she wasted time and tried to distract her confused mind by playing some sort of egg drop game on Yahoo.

10

The sweat slid its way down her back. Kat thought about getting another apple pie, but she knew the only reason it crossed her mind was to delay going closer to Minnesota. It was probably only an hour away. The killer's house (Kat felt guilty calling him the killer in her mind but what was she supposed to do? Call him Don, Donny? Being on a first name basis was not possible) was probably only two more hours past that. Or so the map said.

Kat got in her car pretty much only because she was hot. Inside was no better. It felt like a dry sauna. Rolling all the windows down she cranked the AC and grabbed the map. She didn't know why, it was all planned out and she had gone over it ten times already. She even called ahead and made reservations two towns over at the Days Inn. She wanted to be ready to face the guy being fresh and alert, not tired and worn down from driving all day.

The temperature in the car started to subside a bit and Kat rolled up the windows. Reluctantly, she backed out and headed on the road again. She drove much slower than usual and that was fine, it was early and she was going to have nothing to do but what the small town might offer tonight.

At seven-thirty the sun was still beating hot but now turning the sky brilliant colors of warmness. Kat had checked in. Once again a forgettable room but this time in a not-so-forgettable town. Kat knew she would forget most towns and stops on this trip. In fact she hoped to forget most. But this one was going to stick. Nothing was interesting about it, but the fact that it was only a short drive from Don McAlister would make it unforgettable.

So much for being well rested. Kat didn't sleep one wink in Minnesota. The nerves of what was going to transpire the next day kept her biting her nails all night. Around three she gave up for a while and turned on the light. She kept going over different scenarios in her head. Maybe the guy would be ruined from guilt. The guilt would be enough punishment right, or would it?

Kat remembered hearing a story when she was a kid about a woman whose son was killed by a drunk driver. She had pleaded that the man who hit him wouldn't do jail time. Everyone thought she was crazy, but instead she made a deal. For the next fifty years he had to mail a check made out to her in her son's name for one penny every single week. It had to be post dated and sent on Friday only (the day he was killed). That way the man could never forget what he had done. Every Friday he would have to drop a letter in the mailbox and think about the kid he'd killed.

Kat thought that was a great punishment, since she had learned so much about guilt in the past year. Guilt fueled this whole trip. She wondered if Jasper had died any other way whether she would have done all this? Probably not. But she would never know.

Around quarter of four her eyes felt dry and dusty. She rubbed them and it reminded her of Kyle pleading for water to be poured on his face. Elbows on knees and face in hands Kat sat on the edge of the bed. Her pants draped over the standard desk chair, caught her eye. The letters from Billy were in them. Telling herself she wasn't going to read them, merely put them in her bag, she got up and pulled the folded paper out of the pocket.

The letters didn't make it to her bag, but they did make it back to her bed with her. She snuggled under the blankets and held them on her lap. The lamp next to the bed was spreading just enough light on her hands to read. Unfolding them she checked the mail date and times to put them in order. There was no going back now. She was going to read them.

The first one was short and apologetic. No real feeling or emotions were in it. She could tell he was holding back. A bit disappointed she went on to the second one. It was much longer and deeper. He apologized over and over again until half way through he changed his mind. It went on to say.

You know what? I'm not sorry. I know that might sound cruel but it was the single best kiss I've ever had in my whole life! I replay it over and over again in my mind. Look Kat, I know what it's like to lose the person you love. There is no getting over that, ever. You just learn to deal with it, that's the best you can do. I know it's way too soon for you, but I want you to know I will be there whenever you are ready. Even if you want to be just friends for ten years first. I'm fine with that. I've never felt as good in my life as I did being with you. I want that feeling back. I know we only knew each other for a few short days but...sometimes you can just tell. And don't try to tell me you didn't feel it too. I know you did. I could see it in your eyes. I can't believe I'm being so straightforward. I apologize. It has just been a few days now and I'm in pain needing, to know you're OK. That you don't hate me. Please Kat, please just email, call or just contact me some way to let me know you're all right. You can even call Margaret if you want and let her know. I just need to know.

It went on to apologize again and ended with a formal good-bye, not a personal one like she thought there would be. Finishing it, she thought for a bit. Maybe being friends with him would be fine. Hell, he was three states away right now. There was no chance of anything happening. Right?

The third letter was again short. It was another apology, but this time for the longer apology note that came before it. He went on and said he was sorry if he'd offended her. Kat thought it was cute yet annoying that he apologized so much. The fourth letter made her sit up to re-read it.

Hey again Kat. You must be getting pretty sick of me by now! But this time it's not about you or me, it's about Johnny. I, along with all the other counselors at the camp want to thank you. You were right. Since you left I spent every free second I had at the camp with him. It took a few days but he finally started to open up a bit. He asked about you a lot. Finally he mentioned getting a burn so I talked to the camp nurse and brought him to get examined. Very reluctantly he took off his shirt. Kat you know the night I cried with you was the fist time in years. Well that day in the nurse's office was the second. It was so awful. His entire body was covered with cigarette burns and a few dozen scars from other things. The sick bastards were smart and made sure nothing made a mark past his elbows or below his knees. Well I might be getting in some trouble but I wouldn't let him go home that night. I just couldn't let that happen again. At first he wanted to go home but seemed relieved just the same. I took him right to the courthouse and they are going to let me be his temporary guardian until a foster home is found. He's at the Ranch with me now. You saved this kid a lot of pain and who knows what else Kat. Thank you. Oh and he says hi! Well I better get going, I'm teaching him how to ride. I hope to hear from you soon, so does Johnny.

All thoughts of anything but Johnny and Billy had left her mind. Thankfully. On one hand she was beaming with pride that she'd saved a child from abuse. On the other she was mortified for being right. Knowing there was no logical answer she thought: *How the hell could you do such a thing to a kid? To anyone for that matter?* She wanted to call Billy and thank him for helping but thought better of it since it was four AM. Maybe tomorrow…tomorrow. Best as she could, she kept the thoughts of the ominous day ahead out of her head. Instead she concentrated on Johnny having a better home. With Billy. Finally sleep came and paid her a visit.

11

The morning was rough. She woke up later than planned and felt ready to puke. She knew it was nerves and hunger battling over space in her empty stomach. It took a while for it to settle down. The worst part was her gut screaming for food but her nerves refusing to allow anything in. An hour after getting up she got a vanilla milkshake at the Wendy's across the street. Slowly sipping it made some of the hunger go away. It was the best she could do.

It was almost eleven and Kat had planned to be at his house by ten. A bit behind schedule. No big deal. She figured he would be at work (whatever it might be) until five hopefully. A stakeout was in order: Find the house make the mark and ambush. Well not ambush, just make sure he was home before knocking on the door. But then what next? Scream at him, cry, have tea? She had no clue. Kat just hoped that whatever was right would come out.

Packed and nervous, Kat headed out to find the house in the so-called ghost town. The punk kid at the hotel counter (it seemed lately that she had more conversations with check-in people than anyone else) said it was a *Total Rockin' Ghost town, great for parties…no cops!* For some reason the idea of it being a deserted place made the image of the man look more like a killer.

Kat started her drive by playing loud party music (a stupid CD given to her at some New Year's Eve party four years ago) to try and trick herself into a good mood. Instead of singing along she realized she wasn't even hearing it. Off it went. It was another hot day and Kat opted for the AC. Regardless of whom she was meeting, looking like a sweat-ball wasn't good.

About an hour and a half after leaving the hotel Kat saw a large green sign. The left corner was bent back and both legs were a bit twisted. Heavy dirt and bird shit splattered most of it. Kat read the white letters. *Welcome to Calmare! Founded in 1831 by the miners of Telman Co. Pop. 249.* The nine was falling off but still readable. Kat guessed the population part hadn't been updated in some time.

The lane was narrow and beaten up pretty badly. She could see mountains in the distance and nothingness around her besides trees. A dusty pickup at least thirty years old rumbled by her - blowing black puffs of smoke out the back. The driver had on a cut-off flannel shirt (of course). Kat smiled as it went by way too slowly. When it got next to her it seemed to stop. That's when she realized it was a toothless woman of about thirty, scowling enough to show her brownish gums.

Kat was creeped out but joked to herself that it was the killer's wife. This seemed to ease her tension. According to her Internet map, Raymond Drive should be only two more miles on the left. Up ahead the road looked to be winding, Kat drove slowly. The hairs on the back of her neck started to dance as she took the corner and saw a row of dilapidated old houses. *There was no way anyone could live here!*, Kat thought. Paint (what was left of it) was flaking off the siding. Shutters were on the ground, roofs non-existent or crumbling in. Her guess was that each of these houses were at least over a hundred years old each. From her brief research she assumed that these must be the miners' old houses.

More than once Kat could have sworn she saw movement in a house. But brushed it off to nerves. *Why the fuck couldn't this guy have lived in the city?* Kat bitched to herself. Once again she was the lone car on an empty road. Kat didn't like that. She was craving population. A few yards up ahead a brittle-looking road split off from the crumbling one she was driving on. She stopped before the street to find a sign. Kat saw a pole on the ground and knew she was going to have to get out to read it. Pulling over, she felt the car bumping like a massage chair.

She looked both ways like a good little girl. One car was way off in the distance. Plenty of time to look and get back, she thought. With five fast paces she was across the street and looking at the sign. "*Ra mon Dr ve*" The "y", "d", and "i" were missing but it was definitely the right street. Not what Kat was hoping for. She turned back to cross the street and the car whizzed by her so fast she had to clench her bladder. She could hear laughing from what must have been teenagers fade away, as she hopped back to the car.

Not wanting to, but knowing she'd failed if she didn't, Kat took the sharp left turn onto the dead-looking road. She could only see a little way up the steep drive before it turned and disappeared into the woods. Kat figured it would be just her luck that the only house on the street was a giant haunted mansion run by the crazy Count McAlister. She started up it, her car revved as if it was a kid complaining about having to take a walk instead of being carried.

Higher and higher the road wound up-hill. When the car was reaching close to the over-heat marker, the road leveled out. Both the car and Kat felt relieved. It looked pretty much like the row of abandoned houses below except maybe these where fifty years newer, (but still falling apart). Kat couldn't imagine anyone living here as well and thought the address must have been a mistake. But she kept on looking for number three-sixty-one. The house (which was only half-standing) on her right said one-twelve. She looked down the road and couldn't believe it was long enough to make it up to such a high number. But sure enough the bumpy road took another turn.

This time it revealed a more pleasant looking area. The grass was green (compared to the brown crackly weeds in front of the other houses) and the houses were livable. All three of them. Kat's stomach started to flip (a feeling she was getting used to) seeing it was a dead end. There was no way to stake out this place without standing out like an elephant in a room full of cats. She didn't know what to do. Go down and figure out which house it was? Ring the doorbell now? Leave and come back?

At the entrance to the road she sat in the car. The engine rumbled silently as it tried to cool down from the steep climb. Her eyes went from house to house. Which one? *Which one does the person who ruined my life live in?* Kat questioned. Then, for the second time in fifteen minutes, she had to clench her bladder. This time, not so successfully.

Behind her a loud sharp horn honk blared for a solid five seconds. It was a big grey Cadillac from the eighties.

After composing herself she tried to sneak a glimpse of who the man was. She'd never seen Don McAlister before but the way her heart felt like an over-used pincushion made her know it was him.

12

It took three more honks for Kat to snap out of shock and pull the car to the side of the road. The ominous car pulled up next to her. There was a glare on the window obscuring the view of his face. Kat didn't know if she was happy about that or not. She watched the window roll down in what seemed like slow motion. First she could see the crown of a head with thinning hair. Next, a blotchy forehead with a few moles. The eyes were next, but Kat made a split second decision to look away before they appeared. She didn't want to look into the last pair of eyes to see her husband alive.

Kat was gripping the wheel way too hard. The fake plastic leather squeaked under her wringing hands. She knew the man was going to ask her what she was doing here. He had to, the place was deserted, anyone here had to be suspicious. Lie! She had to lie. How else do you confront someone from another car? If she did he might drive to his house, go in and lock the door forever. But what if she lied and then he found out the truth, he'd never tell anything.

"Can I help you Miss?"

Shit. Shit. Shit. Kat wanted to put the car in reverse, slam on the gas, roll down that damn hill and drive right out of this state. She stared at the wheel. She couldn't look at him.

"HEY! Lady? What are you doing up here?"

Kat turned her head a bit towards him but kept her gaze in the car.

"I'm…look…ing for…Don McAlister." There was a long pause. She knew he was searching his brain to figure out who the Hell she was. Maybe he'd already figured it out from her license plate. She hoped not.

"Who's asking?" He sounded like a convict on the run trying to protect himself. To Kat he was. He should have been arrested. Unless…she stopped her thought. There was no way around this, she had to do it.

"He hit a man a while back in Massachusetts. I'm looking to ask him a few questions." Well, she sounded calm and collected. At least to her own ears. He must have thought she was crazy for not looking at him.

"I was never accused of anything! The fucker ran out in front of the car. He was trying to off himself. What are you, a private investigator?"

Kat had never been hit with anything in her life other than a few kick balls back in Elementary School. Well she now knew what it must feel like to get punched in the face. His comments hit her like a wrecking ball. Her whole body felt tense with pain. Later, she wondered if her muscles all contracted at once bringing the pain or if it was a chemical released from her brain. She wanted to scream at him, telling him he was a fucking liar and that he must be covering his ass.

Before she could even begin to muster up the strength to speak (which would have been a while, it felt like there were three very dry golf balls in her throat stopping her from swallowing and breathing) Don drove off into his driveway. She knew if he got into his house it was all over. Kat coughed up the balls and shook her body as hard as she

297

could to get it back running. His house was the first one, making him only a few yards away. She looked up and saw him slam his car door like he was trying to break it off. He was overweight and wearing a tacky suit. He looked like a regular middle-class man but she knew he wasn't.

Almost forgetting to put the car in park, Kat jumped out and sprinted to the man. He saw her coming and stood his ground. Don put his briefcase on the roof of the car as if he were expecting her to try to tackle him. Having a hundred pounds on her, it was a small possibility she would. But nonetheless he tried to look menacing. Kat stopped a few feet in front of him, out of breath, shaking and ready to puke.

"Look lady! I was never charged with anything or even accused of anything. The stupid fuck must have had one Hell of life to want to go get splattered like he did. You think I liked seeing his guts spill out? Leave me alone!"

The wreaking ball hit once again. This time Kat was standing in an open field with her arms out. The ball hit her full force. She felt acid bubbling in the back of her throat, trying to come out. She couldn't decide if she'd rather that or the golf balls. She wasn't even aware of the sweat that sprung out over her body.

If Don weren't so terrified of who or why this person was here, he would have noticed how horrible she looked. She looked like a woman about to die from the flu. But at the same time, Don was getting many of the same feelings, except he knew how to hide them. After years of having a father yell at him for crying, he'd learn at the age of seven to just bottle up. Don wanted to run and hide. He'd thought it was behind him. His heart had sunk when he'd seen the license plate as he rounded the corner. He knew it had to do with what had happened. What else could it have been? To his knowledge, there had never been a Massachusetts car on the street before, let alone in the state.

And who the hell was this? She was one bad private investigator. For one thing she couldn't even look at him. She hardly even spoke. Maybe it was a friend doing a favor for someone. A reporter? No, that would not make sense. If it was maybe he could tell his story and make it look like he was a sympathetic hero? No. Whoever she was, he just wanted her gone.

Out of all the horrible scenarios that had run through Kat's head (and some were really bad) this one was worse than she could have imagined. She barely got out a word and he was yelling at her about how Jasper had a miserable life and wanted to die. No way, she couldn't believe this, he had to be hiding something.

The two stared at each other's sweating brows. What was next? Who was going to yell at whom? It was like a Mexican stand off with words in place of guns. If words were guns, Don had a machine gun and Kat had one of those toy potato guns kids play with. Don was the one to finally fire first.

"Get the hell off my lawn. There is nothing more to say." He started to turn and walk away. Head down. Kat wasn't sure if it was out of grief, frustration or what. But he sure did look messed up. He even forgot his briefcase.

"I…I just need to know a few things…I'm not here to get you in trouble." Don stopped in his tracks. Only a yard or two from the door. He answered by screaming.

"Look! There is nothing more to know! The guy was fucked up and chose to use me as a way of killing himself. He fucked with me enough as it is. If you want to fuck with someone go yell at his corpse."

This time it was three separate wrecking balls but they were different, they had spikes on them. Kat didn't know what to do. Don slid the key in the lock and opened the door. Stepping in he turned to shut it and Kat spoke one last time.

"I don't need to yell at his body. He's right here."

She pulled out a baggie of ash from her pants pocket. Don looked at her curious and terrified.

"This is all that's left of Jasper Cutter. He was my husband." She held it up high for him to see. Kat wanted to see his face but couldn't through the hot tears that were bubbling out of her lids. What she would have seen was a man fighting back the same hot tears. His lips quivered.

"Maybe if you'd treated him better none of this would have happened. Both our lives would be normal."

The door slammed. His last statement was like the final dramatic twist of the knife in the gut that always killed the bad guy in action movies. Kat felt like the last drop of life she had in her body had just dried up.

13

Shutting the door, Don slammed his forehead against it fighting back tears as best as he could before falling to his knees. This whole accident thing was taking a toll on him. It was a hundred times harder than he'd thought it would be. Looking down at the twisted body he had felt almost nothing, except worry about missing his flight. After a day or so, he'd realized that it was shock that kept him calm that day and that night on the flight back home.

It wasn't until he got to this same spot in his house at three in the morning did he realize he'd killed a man. Don had never had a good life or liked people that much but hurting someone (physically that is, mentally he could kill) never crossed his mind. The worst part of all was the fact that he'd lied. Just as he did now. He regretted telling people that the man committed suicide. The guilt had eaten him apart so much that his wife of nine years was staying at her mother's until he was normal again. Who knew when that would be?

Don had always been a bitter man who used hurtful words. He was definitely his father's son. But since the accident he had been so horrible. Three clients actually got rid of him. That only added more stress to his life. Not like being a chemical waste advisor was any fun anyway. He tried to lie to himself and say he didn't need more clients anyway. The truth was nothing really mattered since he'd taken a life.

Day and night his thoughts were filled with nothing but "the man" (that's what he called Jasper to make him seem less human, just like Kat called him "the killer"). He would wonder non-stop about him, what did he do, did he have kids, a wife (he now knew), what was he like? He would wonder but never really wanted to know. Knowing details would make it much harder. It would make him real and not just a body in the street.

He was tormented by the fact that he'd lied. Would it have been easier to not have? Would his mind be more at ease? NO! Then he would be in jail for manslaughter, lose his wife, his job. That couldn't happen, it would ruin another man's life, his own. Then again things weren't much different now. His wife was gone, he was close to losing his job, and his mind was definitely in jail.

301

How to stop all this and make it better was the only other thing ever on his mind. But he had no answers. Admitting what he had done would be the only way out. But how could jail be better. The guilt would be off his shoulders. And now, now he couldn't believe what he'd just done to the poor man's widow. She had to be horribly upset to drive all the way out here to ask him some questions. Jesus! What had he done? This was his chance. His chance to let it all out. Maybe she would forgive him and not press charges. The damage was already done, what was the use in ruining another life? But after the way he had treated her she might not be so keen on an apology.

Don didn't care. He struggled his weight up and fought the door open. In one giant step he was off the steps and onto the lawn. He hadn't run in twenty years but damn it he'd run now if he had a chance of catching her. But the woman's car was not in sight. He couldn't let her get away.

By far this was the worst Kat had ever felt. Not even the news of Jasper's death was this hard, because now it was all on her shoulders. It *was* her fault. If Don was lying then he had done a good job because she believed him. He looked like he was hurt and messed up from it. Why couldn't it have gone better? Kat barreled down the steep hill without even bothering to touch the breaks. She didn't care anymore.

Killing herself had been an option many times. Now it wasn't, it was a need. But how? That was the only problem. Driving into a tree with no seatbelt would do it (It had to be fast and easy whatever it was). Going down the steep hill would make it so simple to veer off and hit a thick tree. But what if it didn't work and she ended up stuck in a hospital? That would not be acceptable. She needed to find something more definite. Her mind swirled.

I can't believe Jasper actually killed himself. It's too hard to believe...and it was all...because of me. A gun...that would be the best. But too hard to get one. It would take too long. He couldn't have planned it? He had to have just been running... maybe he didn't see the car and it looked like he ran out on purpose. Don't be stupid. NO it is possible. Carbon Monoxide. I think you just fall asleep. But I'll need a garage or something to keep it in the car. The guy could be lying. But why would he? If it was an accident, big deal there is nothing to hide.

Thoughts kept running through her head with no rhyme or reason. She needed to call Patty first. Not to save, her but to thank her and find out what the pizza guy had said to her. She could lie and say she was fine and just wanted to talk. That would work. But really her subconscious wanted to call for a way out. A reason to live. Now that she was the one responsible for Jasper's death, she was *the killer* and she could no longer think of a reason to live.

Booze and pills. That would be the easiest. That was what Patty was going to do. *But Patty didn't kill her husband like I did. She could live with herself, not me. Not after what I did,* Kat thought, until her mind went back to the task at hand. Where the hell was she going to find a place that sold pills and booze in this freaking ghost town?

Once at the end of the street she had a hard time picking right or left. Neither was too promising. Left it was. Hopefully the town would have a liquor and drug store in one. How nice would that be? The speedometer was hitting eighty on the bumpy road. She felt like she was in a rock tumbler. If this road had allowed it, she would have gone faster.

Street after street of abandoned houses lined the way. The thought of other houses hidden behind the rotting ones creeped her out. Why would anyone want to live here? Maybe Don was weirder than she thought? Finally after about as much bumping as she could take she saw the lights of civilization. It was a tiny strip, three maybe five stores. She guessed it was run by locals for locals.

There was a liquor store and, just her luck, a grocery store just across the street. They had to have pills. Liquor store was first. She needed a shot to keep going. She bough two bottles of Absolute Citron. She knew the second bottle wouldn't even be open before she was dead, but she wanted to be safe in case she accidentally dropped something.

Next it was onto the grocery store. The two employees gave her a dirty look that said *"you don't fucking belong here!"* But she thought *Don't worry I won't be here or anywhere for that matter much longer.* It was a mad dash to the medicine aisle. Row after row of pills played with her eyes. Which ones? Kat didn't have a vast knowledge of pills let alone which ones were the best to kill yourself with. She started to read labels and realized that still didn't help.

Narrowing it down to what she thought might work Kat grabbed a bottle of Maximum Strength Excedrin, Stacker 2 weight loss pills (she heard they had an obnoxious amount of caffeine), Sinus and Allergy Relief, and Extra Strength Bayer Aspirin. She had no clue if it would work but hoped so. The lady at the cash register still seemed to hate her. Without trying, they were rude to each other. Kat tossed a fifty at her and said keep the change.

Back in her car Kat opened the Vodka and took a large swig. It stung like fire going down but to her it felt like an end coming near. Placing it between her legs she drove off. The parking lot would not be a good place to do this. Instead she kept driving in the direction she was headed before pulling in. There had to be somewhere she could sneak off to park. Somewhere no one could see the car. The next two miles were deserted. Nothing but the same creepy empty houses. Constantly swigging on the bottle and not wanting to drive anymore she pulled into what used to be a driveway of a half destroyed house. With some complaints from the car Kat gunned the gas to bounce over the tree roots and head into the back yard. There she killed the engine. The street was still visible but most people would ignore a car on the side of the road anyway. They would just pass by here too.

Checking her phone, she was glad (and shocked) it had reception. She still planned on calling Patty but figured she would swallow a bottle or two first so that way she couldn't back out. Like a kid opening Halloween candy, Kat ripped open all the bottles. She poured five or six pills from each bottle in her hand. Ten sounded reasonable to swallow at one time. She shook the pills into her hand and popped ten of them in her mouth followed by an ample amount of vodka. It was a hard swallow, a bit of coughing and choking followed. Maybe ten was too many.

Kat repeated the process (with five pills this time) until she had about half of each bottle gone and a good amount of booze gone. She could already feel the effects of the vodka in her head and her stomach was flipping but not with nerves. She better call Patty before she couldn't talk. Phone in hand, frog pin in other, vodka between legs Kat dialed the number. Waiting for it to ring she glanced over at the passenger seat. It was a mess of cotton puffs, safety seals a few spilt pills and of course the always-smirking grin of Jasper's cookie jar. She was starting to feel guilty, knowing Jasper would be pissed at her for doing this.

"What are you looking at? You did it too. So don't even try to say I'm taking the easy road out…I'm not. I …just… we…" The phone rang once before a voice picked up.

"Yellow!" Instantly by the tone she could tell it was Patty. In spite of the pain in her stomach and bowels she smiled hearing it.

"Patty…"

"Yessss…who is this?"

Kat was about to answer but an air bubble in her chest made sharp pains shoot through her ribs as it tried to make its way out.

"This is Kat…you gave me your frog pin…I was" There was a gasp.

"Girl no need to explain I know who you are. I remember everybody. Especially you sister." Kat felt a warm feeling that she thought was from Patty remembering her but really was the lack of AC and being in closed up car. She was about to open a window for air but then stopped figuring it might help speed up the process. Maybe with heat exhaustion and the rest she'd have a heart attack.

"Sister, are you OK? You're not…are you?" Kat was starting to regret not calling first. She didn't know if she was going to be able to talk long enough to find out what the pizza guy had said. She wanted to know so badly.

"What…wa…how…did "

"Hush yourself! What have you done? Kat tell me where you are and what you've done then I'll tell you what he said. Damn you! Oh God, you sound horrible, you've already done something haven't you? If you called me first you wouldn't be in this situation."

"Pat…It was…my fault he…killed…"

Kat leaned her head back and felt something wet stick to her head. It was her hair. It was the first time she realized that her entire body was sweating not to mention shaking. Her stomach muscles started to tighten and convulse. The inside of her stomach felt like there were ten pissed off cats trying to claw their way out. Then to top it off someone was pouring acid on the cuts. Vomit that tasted like no other puke she had tasted before filled her mouth. It was the oddest thing. It wasn't like throwing up it sort of just crawled into her mouth. She never even leaned forward to let it spill out. Instead it just flowed over her teeth and lips before dribbling on to her breasts.

"LISTEN to me Kat. Hang up and call and ambulance. I don't care where you are sister I'll come and take care of you for a week. I'll make you all better but first you have to call 911." Her body was becoming weak and she couldn't even tell that the phone was next to her head. Her arms felt paralyzed, as did most of her body. Carefully using her tongue she thrust out the vomit in her mouth to speak.

"I'm...sawwyy." Breathing was getting harder. That's when Kat realized she didn't even think to leave a note. Oh well who would read it anyway besides Val. Maybe Billy. It was no use now. The shaking and spurts of vomit that kept coming up were uncontrollable. The vodka fell from her lap. As much as she wanted to clean her mouth with it she couldn't find the energy to grab it. She could hear soft crying on the other end of the line, though it was starting to fade. She couldn't tell if it was her or if Patty was talking lower.

"Kat...at least tell me where you are."

"Go...na...see me...huban."

The rotted tree swing she had been staring at had bright flashes of light in front of it. For some strange reason they made her think of pixies and her childhood. Having that flashback in her mind made her wonder when her life was going to flash before her eyes. But it didn't. She tried to think of Jasper but her mind was getting so foggy. His face was barley visible in her mind's eye.

"Kaaaaaaaaaat…" She heard the voice talking still but couldn't understand it. She dropped the phone and didn't even know it. Slowly she started to slump to the right getting closer and closer to Jasper. Tunnel vision was taking over. Darkness was coming around from all sides. Her mind didn't work anymore, she didn't even try to fight it. The darkness won. The phone laid on the hump in between the sides. Patty was still crying and talking even though Kat could no longer hear.

"Listen sister…the least I can do is tell you what Vincent said…that was his name Vincent…he told me…"

Darkness. Nothing but darkness.

14

The light was as bright as she had expected. Brighter than anything she'd ever seen. Her hearing was not what she thought it would be, it was muffled and awkward. She couldn't see a thing except blurred figures that must have been angels. She started to panic wondering how the hell she could get into Heaven. Ever since her mother died she'd denounced religion. She couldn't believe it was real. That's when she felt the tube. Well one of them at least.

It was coming from her nose and going around her ears. *Fuck.* Another one (which was sore) was jammed into her right wrist. *Shit.* Wristband, gown, her vision started to clear. It was a hospital. No heavenly light, no angels. She was still on earth in her own Hell. Now she was going to have to live (not long if she could help it) with the embarrassment of having tried to kill herself. Wait a second. How the hell did she get here from hiding behind a decrepit old house in a ghost town?

Everything was getting clearer. She was noticing how bad her throat was. It felt like the cats that were in her stomach had made their way up there and had a field day. It was so bad she did her best not to move it in any way. Her belly wasn't much better. The muscles were sore as Hell and she knew sitting up was impossible. The one thing she did want to do was block the light that was in her eyes. She went to put her hand up but it wouldn't move.

Wondering if it was her mind not being able to move her hands she tried again. It moved but only an inch until she felt plastic (at least that's what she guessed it was) bite into her arm. She was tethered. They really didn't trust her. Second by second things got clearer. The beeping of the heart monitor started to blip in her ears. She wanted to yell for someone to tell her what the hell was going on or more importantly how did she get here? But that was impossible.

It seemed like an eternity waiting for a nurse to come check on her. She could see a big pitcher of water that was so cold it had beads of sweat racing down the sides. Her throat was so dry it would be Heaven to gulp it down. For a minute she knew how Kyle must have felt with his eyes.

Then an angel walked in (Hell, at this point anyone walking in would have been sent from Heaven). Nurse Jessica strutted in with a wiseass smile as if saying "*ha-ha you didn't kill yourself after all!*" or at least that is how Kat interpreted it.

"You're a very lucky woman Mrs. Cutter!" Kat wanted to say *like hell I'm not!* But her damaged throat wouldn't let her. She gave back the same smile the nurse came in with.

309

"No, you really are. Most people don't survive ingesting what you did. You're lucky he found you when he did."

Who? Who? How? Kat screamed inside her head. The nurse produced a plastic spoon out of nowhere and removed the lid off the pitcher. Kat looked like a dog about to get a treat. She puckered her lips out begging for whatever was inside. The spoon plunged in and back out to reveal several chips of ice. Kat couldn't think of anything she'd ever wanted more. Nurse Jessica slid them off the spoon and into her gaping mouth. They felt wonderful. Who knew ice could be such a delicacy?

Kat didn't like the way the woman looked. She was young, with the heavy accent of the area, had an engagement ring, and had the air of someone who thought they knew everything. *Well you don't know shit about me* Kat once again yelled in her empty head. But the same time that she hated her she loved her for giving her ice. It was torture, having a million questions and not being able to speak.

Jessica said nothing as she fed ice chips to Kat like a Mom feeding chicken soup to a young child. After five or so spoons Kat felt the water hit her stomach. They did not agree with each other. She must have done some major damage down there. By the time the sixth spoon was heading for her Kat turned her head. Jessica stood up and said.

"I'll go get the doctor and counselor."

Kat did not want to deal with some hoity toity doctor telling her he knew what she was going through and that everything would be all right. She knew it wasn't going to be.

Within a minute of the prissy nurse leaving, Kat realized that she was the only one in the room, it was a private room. Then a man and woman entered. It looked like a sketch from a sitcom. The woman was at least a foot and a half taller than the man. Kat smirked. The two introduced themselves, she didn't get their names and didn't really care either. She did understand that the woman was the doctor and the man was the quack.

Kat rolled her eyes and stared at the ceiling like a defiant child as the doctor explained the damage she'd done to herself and the therapy and medication she was going to have to take. Kat had never been rude like this before but she was pissed to be alive. All the hurt and guilt was still there. After making a few notes and checking a few vitals it was the shrink's turn to blab.

The shaved head, goatee-wearing midget (well probably 5'3") hopped up on the edge of her bed as if he were an old buddy. Even though she knew it was probably an old technique to get people comfortable with him, it still worked. At least it drew her attention. He said "Hi" and went about removing the restraints around her wrists. She was definitely going to like this guy better, even if it was all plotted out.

The middle-aged man set down his clipboard and looked deeply into Kat's eyes. It was so long that Kat started to smile (she would have laughed if she could). Finally he looked away to the doctor and gave her a nod to leave. She looked kind of annoyed, but obliged.

"Katharine, may I call you Kathy?" Kat shook her head no. With her newly freed wrists she lifted her arm and wrote *K-a-t* in the air with the index finger. He nodded and began again.

"Kat, I've been doing my job for some time now. I'm not a cocky man but I do believe I'm very good at it. I can look at most people and see that they don't want to die. From there I can usually get them to love life again. Yes it takes time but it works."

Kat was wondering where he was going with this. Looking at him, she felt safe. Not as if he was here to protector her, but as in she could open up and talk to this guy about major feelings way.

"Then there are the other ones. When I look in their eyes I know they want to die. With them it takes years if ever to get back to society. But what I see in your eyes is the rarest. I see it almost never." She couldn't tell if he was putting her on or not. She sure hoped not.

"I can tell Kat that you want to die because you feel like you should. Not because you want to. There is a tremendous guilt that is too much to handle. If we can get over that, your life will be OK." "Holy Shit" Kat thought. He was good. She hadn't even thought about that. It was true though. It was the guilt. He went on and talked for a while asking her yes and no questions. He got her smiling.

After a half hour or so he got her some paper and a pen so she could ask some questions. Her first one was: *How did someone find me?* Dr. Kane (which she finally noticed on his name tag after a while) smiled big. "Well I'm going to let him explain it to you. Now at first I thought it would have to wait a few weeks after we'd had a few sessions, but I think you can take it. But you must first understand why. Just let him speak and explain everything."

Kat's smile was completely gone. She had a feeling of who it had to be. Her tortured stomach did one of its brilliant flips it had come so accustomed to. The doc reassured her again then left the room. Five minutes later he entered.

It was as if he was trying to get a little boy to meet a new friend. He stood at the door comforting whoever it was. Then slowly Kat saw it was who she was dreading. Don McAlister.

His face was puffy and red which had to be from hard tears. Kat found herself pushing back into her bed as if with just the right amount of pressure, she would sink back and disappear in it. Doctor Kane saw this and rushed to her side to reassure her. He whispered in her ear, and Kat seemed to ease up a bit. Don wrenched a handkerchief in his hands over and over.

"As you know Kat, this is Don." Her face scrunched up with hatred.

"Now usually for a meeting like this to happen it would take weeks of building up to it. But I think you're both strong enough. Also what needs to be said could solve everything right here and now." Kat's wrinkled up face smoothed out to interest. *What the hell could he possibly have to say? A little while ago he accused me of Jasper's death. He must have followed me after I left?* Kat's thoughts ran on as Don stared at the floor turning his knuckles white and red twisting and twisting the red rag.

The doctor slowly coaxed Don out of his shell. He still wouldn't look at her but his mouth opened to speak.

"I...I'm sorry I yelled at you. I was just...so scared."

If that was all he was here for he could forget it. Kat was glad her voice was gone because it would get her in some trouble right now.

"It...was all a... lie."

Don started to cry, putting his face in the already wet and gooey handkerchief. The doctor pulled up a chair for him but kept it at the end of the bed so he wouldn't have to get too close. Don plunked down his weight on it. It slid back a few inches with a harsh scrapping noise that made all three of them wince. Kat was trying to figure out what he meant by "a lie". Don slowed his tears just enough to talk.

"All of it. I don't know why I yelled at you. I'm so sorry. It's been so hard. I've had to live a lie. Even to my wife. I've never done that." He took a second to breathe, as Dr. Kane rubbed his shoulders as if he was a boxing champ in-between rounds. Kat wanted to scream "*AND*"?

"Your husband didn't just run out in front of my car…it was my fault he died. I was looking for a file on a certain company when I pulled out. I didn't even look up until it was too late. He tried to leap out…of the way. I couldn't… stop." Kat didn't know what to feel. Joy? Hatred for the man? What? She needed to calm herself and hear it all before she reacted.

"He was already dead…when the cops came…I thought…what's confessing that it was my fault going to do? It wouldn't change anything. Why ruin my life as well?"

Kat couldn't believe what she was hearing. All this guilt this whole time, because he'd "lied".

"But I was wrong. I've never been a chipper guy…after that I was miserable. I tried to act like nothing was wrong. I even tried to lie to myself and say he did do it on purpose. But it didn't work. I knew the truth. I killed a man and lied about it."

Dr. Kane was watching Kat's face to judge her reaction. It was blank. Nothing. He was worried that she might go into a mental shock. Don was over the hump and didn't need him for comfort any more. Kat did now. He went to her side and scooped up her hand. Kat hardly flinched.

Don was going to keep speaking but the doctor held up a finger to tell him to hold on. He said Kat's name. She didn't respond. The third time he said it she reluctantly turned to him.

"Are you alright? I know this is a lot. But you can stop feeling guilty now." Kat nodded her head and went back to staring at the man who'd killed her husband. She caught him looking at her. Immediately he looked away. The doctor told him to go on.

"My life has been falling apart ever since. Then yesterday, I saw you and got scared. When you mentioned his name I just panicked. That's how I've always dealt with things. I'm not the nicest person in the world. But I'm not horrible. Soon as you left I ran outside to stop you and apologize but you were gone. I drove around trying to find you and that's when I saw your bumper sticking out from one of the old houses on Hempstead Ave."

Figures, Kat thought. *The man who took away my husband's life saves mine.* Her brain was still trying to process the overwhelming information. She looked to Kane as if to ask what to do.

"It's OK Kat. It's OK." Her gaze landed on the ceiling.

"I'm…so sorry Mrs. Cutter. I know you probably want me dead and will never forgive me but I already feel much better for doing this. If you want I will go to the police in Massachusetts and tell them what happened. I'll serve my time. Anything. Anything to help."

Kat ever so slightly shook her head "No". Even though he'd put her through a long slow Hell and took away her husband it was still an accident. And by saving her life he had made amends. They all understood that this was her way of saying it was over. Don stood up and backed up a bit.

"Thank…thank you." Don whispered. The relief on his face made him look much younger and healthier than when he entered the room. He backed out and the doctor nodded to him.

"I'm proud of you Kat. You handled that very well. Do you want to be alone or do you want to talk now?"

Kat closed her eyes and turned her head away. Dr. Kane left silently.

PART SIX
A NEW SEASON

1

A week and a half later Kat was still in the hospital, but speaking fine. The first week she didn't speak at all. She filled her journal up with so many thoughts, that only a few pages remained blank. It turned out to be a great therapy tool. Now knowing all the staff, Kat was pretty much ready to be released as soon as she could hold down food a bit better. Each day she would meet with Dr. Kane. The therapy part was pretty much over now, so they would use the hour to chat. Kat had felt amazing after Don had admitted what had happened. Of course it didn't bring back Jasper, but it did ease all the pain and suffering she was going through thinking he'd killed himself.

Kat realized that the whole trip had been fueled by guilt. She was fine with that and vowed to finish what she'd set out to do anyway. Dr. Kane also thought it would be a good idea (as long as she stayed away from stalkers). The doctor even helped her deal with the Kyle incident. But what helped most of all was that he convinced her there was a life worth living when she finished. He was straightforward and told her it was going to be hard. Some days would be better than others. Kat felt a debt of gratitude to the doctor and knew she would keep in touch with him when she was out.

Not finding any personal contact info when Kat was admitted, they had called no one to tell them where she was. That was fine with her. She planned on letting no one know about this. Not for a while at least. Maybe when she was older she might see someone who looked like they needed to hear the story.

The first person Kat called was not Val, but Patty. She felt horrible leaving her thinking she was dead. In fact she couldn't even remember most of the conversation. The phone rang. She was nervous about getting a tongue-lashing or worse, Patty refusing to talk to her for scaring her to death.

"Yellow!" Kat hesitated, not sure what to say first.

"Don't hate me."

"I'm sorry…who…this isn't?"

"It's Kat…I'm alive." She heard a sharp inhale and what sounded like dry sobs. Not waiting for a response Kat started to explain what had happened and apologized profusely.

"So that's what happened. Please don't hate me."

"Sister…I can't hate someone for that. You know damn well I was in that situation once too. I was just lucky as were you." The two talked for a long while, feeling like old friends. Patty told her to stop by anytime she was ever in town and to give her a ring now and again, but right before hanging up, Kat confessed.

"You know Patty you actually did save my life before. Many times probably. Every time I thought about it, your pin and you popped in my mind. I can't thank you enough."

Patty responded with a sigh of flattery.

"You still haven't told me what the pizza guy said. I know you said you began to but I didn't hear it. Would you tell me know? I've been dying to know for so long."

Patty chuckled.

"Dear, I pray to God that you will never know it. For that would mean you never had another moment of weakness in your life."

2

In her last session with Dr. Kane, they sat at his desk hunched over a road map. Together they planned the perfect route to catch up on the states back East she'd missed, then hit the West Coast again and finally finish up in Texas. With a thick red marker Kat traced it out. They figured two to three months would do it. Kane made her promise that this time the trip would be enjoyable, not a mission. He printed her out interesting facts and visitor areas on twenty-three of the last twenty-five states (Hawaii and Alaska she wasn't worried about yet. Finish the country first, then she'd see about those).

On her release day Dr. Kane walked Kat to her car. They hugged and again she promised to keep in touch. After she got in and closed the door he knocked on the window so she would roll it down. She looked up curiously at him. From his lab coat he pulled a small little package.

"What's this?"

"A little going away present."

Kat was touched, never had she met a doctor so concerned with a patient. The night before he had even taken her to meet his wife and two daughters. They'd had dinner and went to a movie.

"I can't thank you enough Doc, you didn't have to get me anything."

"Yeah but I knew you would really appreciate it."

Kat wanted to open it with him there but he walked away with a big smile and a wave. He was one of those people you wished you could put in your pocket and pull out whenever you needed them, Kat thought as she watched him disappear back into the building. Not wanting to wait, she tore the brown paper off the small box to reveal an odd looking necklace.

It looked like a crystal but it was hollow and see through. She read the back of the box. In fancy cursive print it said: *Keep your loved one close to your heart always.* Inside, on a beautiful silver necklace hung the round diamond cut crystal. She grasped it and unscrewed. It came off the necklace. Peering inside of it Kat realized it might fit one half baggie of Jasper's ash. It was wonderful! Without wasting time, she snagged a bag out of her fateful companion's half hollow inside.

As if she were pouring TNT, Kat let the ash gently fall into the crystal. Not one spec was spilled. She was right - about half of it fit. Screwing back on the necklace she was amazed at how it now sparkled with an almost purple hue. She slipped it around her neck. It was comfortable. Kat could see herself wearing this for a long time, if not forever.

A few days after adjusting to the real world, Kat called Val for the first time since leaving the ranch. She felt horrible for not letting her know she was all right but she was better now. Calling her daily would be just fine. No answer at her house phone. Odd she was always home at this time. She called her cell next. After four rings she answered in mid laugh.

"Hello?"

"Hi Val."

"Kat, Baby?" She could hear her shushing people to hear better.

"Jesus Honey! You've had all of us a nervous wreck!"

All of us? Kat wondered.

"I'm really sorry Val. A lot has happened. I wanted to call but couldn't. But don't worry I'm OK now and I promise to call everyday." She could hear voices still in the background. Kat thought they seemed a bit familiar and wondered if she was at a faculty meeting.

"Where are you?" Val didn't respond.

"Sweetie someone wants to say hi to you." Kat was totally confused when a deep trembling voice said "Hello" quietly.

"It's Billy." Kat was now more confused than she'd ever been. But it didn't matter, her heart started to race, knowing it was him. She did feel it, that wonderful feeling. A smile crept across her face.

Kat was on the phone for three and a half hours that night. The phone was passed back and forth from Val to Buck to Margaret, to Billy, even Trevor (who Kat learned was the reason Val was in Arkansas again). But what surprised her the most was hearing a tiny voice speak her name. Johnny thanked her and said he wanted to see her again. When he said good-bye he even made a kissing noise.

She caught up with all of them but told them nothing of what had happened to her. No use in telling it. None of it mattered now. What mattered now was she was fine. And was going to be fine. For the first time since the whole ordeal had started Kat saw herself with a future. She might not know what it was but it was there nonetheless.

Kat went to bed smiling that night. She was excited for this new trip to start. She promised herself to hit every cheesy tourist trap there was and to take her time to enjoy it. The ashes were secondary this time. Her poor stomach bubbled once again, making it hard to fall asleep. But it was OK this time, butterflies of excitement caused the bubbles.

On the table in Kat's room, next to Jasper's jar, the map was laid out. There was a new three-inch line of fresh red ink leading from Texas to Arkansas.

ABOUT THE AUTHOR

Mike was born and raised in Western Massachusetts, then moved to New York City to study film directing. With an Associate's Degree in Teleproduction and a Bachelor's Degree in Film Directing, Mike co-founded AloeRice Pictures, a New York based production company. Mike has written and directed several live action super-hero shows, and is the writer and director of several highly acclaimed short films. Currently, he is working on two new novels which will be released soon. The author welcomes your comments and invites you to keep up with his current projects by visiting: www.AloeRice.biz

Printed in the United States
30417LVS00001B/43-111

9 781420 824438